BEATING THE BRIDGE

MAKE CHOICES THAT EMPOWER AND INSPIRE

Sara

BY SARA B. WOLF

Copyright © 2010 Sara B. Wolf
All rights reserved.
ISBN: 1450555357
EAN13: 9781450555357

Special thanks to Colleen Lockwood,
Cover artist and lifelong friend

When the world says, "Give up,"
Hope whispers, "Try it one more time."

~Author Unknown

Contents:

Introduction 3

Chapter 1: A Shot in the Toe 7

Chapter 2: The Right Path 19

Chapter 3: I Run for Life 33

Chapter 4: I Dreamed a Dream of Running 47

Chapter 5: Half a Soul 63

Chapter 6: A Little Sausage 75

Chapter 7: No Victims 85

Chapter 8: The Voice Inside 95

Chapter 9: It's Just a Rock 105

Chapter 10: On the Way to Ballet 115

Chapter 11: Where There's Smoke, There's Fire…men 127

Chapter 12: A Call to Action 139

INTRODUCTION

On October 25, 2009, I crossed over a bridge in Washington, DC. It was not a very long bridge or a famous bridge. It was not a steep or rickety bridge. It was just an ordinary bridge. But it happened to be at mile 20 of the 26.2-mile Marine Corps Marathon. The day had been years in the making, and many obstacles had stood between this dream and me. I had fallen down and risen back up again countless times on the long journey toward this day. Even as I stood at the start line that morning, I was not convinced that I would make it to the bridge in time. I only knew that I had made it this far, and I had to give it my very best effort. And now I was crossing over a bridge at 1:07 P.M. with 20 miles behind me and 6.2 more miles to go. I passed a sign that said *Beat the Bridge*. You see, to be allowed to finish the entire course of the marathon, all participants were required to reach this particular bridge within a certain time frame. It just so happened that you had to be there by 1:15 P.M. I crossed the bridge with eight minutes to spare.

I was beating the bridge because years earlier I had made an Empowering Choice to run that marathon, reach that bridge, cross over it in time, and get my medal. I had made an Empowering Choice, and I was willing to pay any price and climb any mountain to get there. And I did pay, believe me. I did not give up, and I refused to quit. And it was worth all the effort, too. When I crossed that bridge, I knew that all of the hard work, persistence, determination, and passion with which I pursued this goal were paying off. I said to myself, "Right here, right now, I belong in this moment. I am exactly where I am supposed to be. I am "beating the bridge."

A bridge is defined as a structure built to span a physical obstacle such as a road or body of water, for the purpose of providing passage over the obstacle. In my case, the bridge itself was the obstacle. Everyone has bridges—obstacles that must be faced and overcome. Everyone has his or her own bridge. I made a Choice that Empowered me and Inspired me to reach my bridge and cross over it.

What is your bridge?

CHAPTER 1:
A SHOT IN THE TOE

"You're going to put that shot *where*?" I exclaimed, my head bowed and my eyebrows raised, as I watched the podiatrist direct a long needle toward the big toe on my left foot. But let me back up for you a moment.

In 2003, I went to a podiatrist for an ingrown toenail. I was twenty-six-years-old and had been an avid runner for several years. For some months, that toenail and surrounding skin had been red, swollen, and irritated. I could feel it pulsing during my daily three-mile run, after which I would remove my sneaker, hoist up my leg into a yoga position, and pick at it. Using clippers, I would try to dig the nail out but only succeeded in causing more anger and aggression in the toenail. It was just too enticing not to prod and poke at it, you understand, rather like a pimple that begs to be popped. So, I finally gave in to the advice of others, not the least of which was my mother, and made the appointment with the podiatrist.

I sat in the exam room chair, and he confirmed that the nail was most assuredly very angry and displeased with my recent invasive actions. He spoke casually and nonchalantly regarding this exceptional problem I was having that was now interfering with my daily life and routines, as though he were discussing what to have for dinner that night.

"Oh, yes. I can take it out. No problem. It's a quick and easy in-office procedure. You'll be back on your feet and running loops in the park in no time."

Fabulous, it sounded like no big deal whatsoever. He went on to explain that he would simply numb the area, take out the nail, and bandage the toe. He would give me instructions for changing the dressing and send me off with a little pain medicine.

"Pain medicine?" I asked.

"Oh, well some patients experience some slight discomfort after the numbness wears off, but it will be fine. It will heal quickly. I do this all the time."

Famous last words. Did I think to ask what the "numbing" would involve? You would think that would be an obvious question to ask, but the doctor was so confident and nonchalant that it didn't cross my mind to ask it. He does this everyday, after all. He had caught my attention with the mention of pain medication, so I was somewhat distracted by the possibility of pain *after* the procedure. I therefore did not stop to consider pain *before* the procedure. I suppose I assumed the numbing agent would be in the form of a topical cream or ointment. Either way my toenail problems would soon be a thing of the past. I made the appointment.

A week later I showed up at the office with my mother at my side. At my earlier visit, the nurse had told me to bring someone to drive me home, as the toe would be all bandaged up for a day or so, and I might not be up to driving myself. So my mother sat in the waiting room with a magazine, and I went back to a treatment room. A nurse came in and told me to remove my shoes and sit on the table. She handed me a clipboard with papers attached.

"Don't worry about it honey," the nurse said. "Those are just papers giving the doctor permission to do the procedure. You sign and date it at the bottom."

I skimmed the papers so quickly that I cannot tell you anything that was written on them. I simply gave myself over to the capable hands of experience, assured that there was nothing to fear. I didn't think twice about signing these papers—I merely accepted without question that this was something that needed to be done. It was a procedure that the doctor had performed hundreds, maybe even thousands of times before and probably does on a daily basis. All of my ingrown woes and toe picking would soon be over, and my toe and I could live happily ever after. So I signed and gave my permission to do what was necessary. The giving of my permission is a very important point that is directly related to the idea of Empowering Choices, so hang on to that thought.

I sat on the table with my foot stretched out before me, and the nurse readied all of the instruments and the supplies. The doctor came in and said that he would numb the toe for the procedure by inserting a little shot with the numbing agent to deaden the nerves.

"A shot?" This is unexpected. I began to worry. "Umm, is that going to hurt?"

"Some people find it uncomfortable," he replied. "But after you have the shot, you will not feel a thing."

Uncomfortable? *Some* people? Okay, I can deal with that. It will only last a moment, and it's not like I've never had shots before. I have blood drawn all the time, and I have had enough Novocain in my life to numb a horse. No big deal. Be a big girl. You're an adult.

Now let me just describe this for you. The needle is inserted into your big toe. For some, I need not give any more details, but it bears repeating. The needle is actually inserted *into* your big toe! Not just on the surface, mind you, but deep within to get to the nerve. The needle is *not* pulled out at that point, as you are writhing in pain, but is inserted *deeper* still to get to the bottom nerves. It is rather like throwing salt on a wound! I actually thought the needle was going to come poking out the other side of my toe! I have never in my life experienced such excruciating and terrifying pain. I will never forget the agony. Perhaps I'm being overly dramatic in my retelling of the experience, but I think not. Pain, anguish, torture, and suffering—that's what stands out about this experience.

Fast-forward one year. Same toe. Same nail. Same doctor. You would have thought that I had learned my lesson the first time. But apparently, ingrown toenails tend to be a recurring theme—nails continue to grow, after all. Perhaps you knew this, but I sure didn't. Despite the assurance that the procedure the previous year would take care of the problem, it was back. And the doctor was now ready for round two, the sequel.

"Well, you see doctor," I explained in a calm, cool, and collected tone. "I have the slightest bit of apprehension about that because, umm, well, how shall I put this? It hurt like a son of a #*@!*"

He suggested that I take a medication beforehand that would not render me unconscious, but put me in a very dopey, drowsy, *happy* state of mind. It would assuredly ease my worry and calm my nerves, so that the experience would not be quite so uncomfortable for me. *Uncomfortable* is not the word I would use to describe it, doc.

Okay, this sounded like a reasonable, valid, and suitable suggestion. A happy pill would calm my fears and my nerves. It would put me in a state of bliss and enhance my calm feelings. After all, it wasn't so bad, was it? Yes, it hurt, but in hindsight, was the pain and agony really so terrible? I am strong. I am a woman. Bring it on. Unfortunately the nerves down in my big toe did not quite get that memo! Pain, agony, anguish, suffering, tears, and screams! Yeah, doctor, it was still just a slight bit uncomfortable.

You are not going to believe this, but I swear it is true—a year or so later, I found myself in the office of another podiatrist. Unbelievable. I sat in the office, waiting, waiting, waiting, nervous, and scared. What if I have another ingrown toenail? What if I have to get that shot again? How am I possibly going to face the pain that is in store for me? Memories of my previous procedures returned and filled me with dread and fear. It was then that I had a revelation. It was a light bulb moment—one of those flashes when an astoundingly simple solution occurs to you. A solution so incredibly basic that you can't believe it did not occur to you before. I had a thought that suddenly just appeared in my head:

I will not have that shot in my toe ever again.

I sure liked the sound of that. I said it out loud to the empty room to hear it echo off the walls. I repeated it several times for dramatic effect. "I will not have that shot in my toe ever again." Not ever. No matter what. From now, today, and every day until the day that I die, I will never ever have to experience that again. I had made a decision and put my foot down (not too hard!) I made a choice. See this foot? See this toe? No shot in this toe or any toe on these feet. Not now. Not ever.

The foot doctor walked into the exam room just then. He greeted me with a friendly smile and handshake, just as nice as you please, ready to assist and be helpful in any way he possibly could.

"Now, young lady, what seems to be bothering you today."

"I will not have that shot in my toe ever again. Ever. No matter what," I replied.

"No shots in the toe" was my first conscious Empowering Choice. No doubt, I had made many choices in my life, both Empowering and not. But when I said those words to myself in that doctor's office something happened. An enormous weight was lifted off my shoulders, and a great burden was removed from my mind and my soul. Of course, I would take any and all actions necessary to ensure the health and happiness of my toes and feet, addressing any foot issues that might arise now or in the future. But no matter what, those issues would not result in a treatment or procedure that required that shot because I made a choice. Nobody can hold me down and force me to have that shot. These are my feet, it's my toe, and it's my choice. I felt a tremendous sense of empowerment. I am in control! I have control over my own body, and I can make choices about my health and wellness. I can make choices about my own future, and I can stand by them and see that they're honored. I can shout them from a mountaintop. I can agree with doctors and follow their guidance. I can disagree with them, and I can get another opinion. I can get twenty more opinions, or I can do nothing. I have that choice, and it is my right and responsibility to make choices for myself. I am responsible for my health, happiness, and contentment. When I chose never to experience that procedure, I felt an inner strength and security. It was as if my soul was shining inside of me, reaching out, and taking charge of the situation. I was taking matters into my own hands, and I was ensuring safety and security for my future and myself. Never again would I have to worry about a shot in the toe. Never again would I have to face the pain and suffering.

As I was arming myself with my Empowering Choice and feeling my renewed security and comfort, something very important occurred to me that I had completely forgotten. I had signed a form! The first time I went to the podiatrist to have the ingrown toenail removed, I had signed a permission form for the procedure. The Empowering Choice had always been in my hands. I could have refused to sign that document and sought another form of treatment or another method of sedation. I had the option, choice, and responsibility to seek other opinions, ask a thousand questions if I wanted to, or to do nothing at all and simply live with the toenail as it was. I had the choice, but I just had not recognized it, even though it was written in black and white which I readily, unquestionably, and trustingly signed my name to.

We make decisions in life. We make choices—some are big and some are small. Pizza or hamburger? Action movie or romantic comedy? Dog or cat? Jeans or pants? Stay home or go out? Baseball or football? Run or walk? Beach vacation or ski vacation? Community college or university? Liberal arts major or journalism? Online dating or singles parties? Get married? Have children? Quit my job? Move to another city? Take this suggested medication despite the possible side effects? Go back to school for another degree? Buy a house? Run a marathon? We make decisions every day, and our choices affect our lives, our future, and the lives of those around us. As children, we decide what sport we want to play, what video game to play, which friend to hang out with, and whether to obey the rules or misbehave. As adolescents, we decide whether to hang out with a particular crowd, study for the test, do our homework, sneak out past curfew, or give in to peer pressure or stand firm. As adults, we must choose a career, a lifestyle, a partner, how to spend our money, and how to spend our time. Sometimes the decisions are easy because the choice seems obvious and straightforward. Sometimes it's as simple as right versus wrong—the right thing versus the selfish thing. Sometimes the choices are difficult, and we do what is right but not what is easy. Sometimes we take the path of least resistance. Sometimes our decisions are influenced by others or the way we were brought up. For whatever reason, we make the decisions that we do, and we must live with the consequences of our choices.

Often we don't recognize how important a decision is when we make it; only in hindsight do we realize how momentous the decision was. Subsequently, we can't help but wonder how our life might have turned out if we had chosen a different path. What if my family had stayed in Ohio and not moved to Texas when I was a teenager? What if I had gone to the University of Houston and not the University of Texas? What if I had scored only several points lower on that exam and not gotten into college at all? What if that drunk person with whom I got the ride home had not been so lucky? What if my best friend's parents had not purchased the home two doors up from mine, and we had never met? Of course, we can consider the what ifs of our lives forever.

Choices are something that each of us must face in life. Sometimes they are under our own control, and sometimes others make them for us. So how are Empowering Choices different from regular ordinary life choices? What is so Empowering about them? What does it really mean to be Empowered? Can I change my own future and my destiny through Empowering Choices? Once you have made an Empowering Choice, can you go back and change your mind? How do you stick with the Empowering Choice once you have made it? How might it affect your friends and loved ones? How can I make Empowering Choices that will positively influence my happiness, peace of mind, and success in life?

When I said, "I will not have that shot in my toe ever again," I felt a stronger sense of Empowerment in my soul then I had ever felt before. I took control of my own destiny and stood up for myself. There is one thing that I can recommend to you for certain—if you ever find yourself in a podiatrist's office, I *do not* recommend a shot in the toe!

CHAPTER 2:
THE RIGHT PATH

You are walking on a path through a forest. It is the path that you have set out on in life, and there are wondrous and enchanting sights, sounds, and smells all around you. Occasionally you have others walking with you, perhaps leading you or maybe pushing you from behind or just walking beside you and sharing the moment. But this is your path and yours alone. It is not the path of your parents, spouse, or friend. Their paths may intersect yours or run parallel for a stretch, but each person has his or her own path. You are born to yourself, you live with yourself, and you die with yourself. Ultimately and more often than not, you walk your path alone. The path is not smooth—it has tangled twists and sharp turns. It has bumps and detours. The feelings of wonder and awe that you experienced at the beginning, when you were a child, are replaced with responsibility and perhaps even fear. There are questions in your mind about which is the right path. Must you walk alone? Could you have a sunnier, brighter path like that guy over there? You may wonder if it's too late to switch paths or grow weary and wish to stop and rest along the way. But there is one thing for certain—you must press on and must not turn back. You must keep in a forward motion, whether you are running with happiness and confidence in the direction of the future, walking with contentment, or barely crawling with weariness and sorrow. You must keep going down the path toward the future, breathing, growing, learning, changing, and living. Most importantly, you must continue to make choices. This is what it is to be alive.

For some people, the twists and turns in their path will become too much for them to handle. The dark forest all around seems too scary, or they cannot bear having to walk the path alone. Lacking the self-confidence and determination or basic life skills to press on, they will seek a crutch. We all use crutches once in a while. It is normal and natural. The problem occurs when the crutch is needed and necessary for any forward motion to continue. A crutch takes many forms-alcohol, drugs, a need for attention, or reliance on a person who may not have your best interest at heart. Some people recognize their dependence on a crutch and take solid steps to rid themselves of it so that they can walk down their path on their own two feet. There are others who rely so heavily on their crutch that they either lean on it throughout their lives or their path ends prematurely as a result of it.

As I am walking down my path, I look behind me to see how far I have come. I see that I stood tall and firm through the bumps and detours, and I pressed on through wind and rain. I smiled in the sunshine and learned lessons from the shade. As I look back on my journey, my confidence, security, and self-assurance grow and blossom inside me. I am proud of how far I have come and walk forward toward a future that is uncertain and unclear but full of hope and opportunity.

I am moving merrily along, when I come to a fork in the road. My path divides into two directions. One path will lead me down one stretch of road and the other path will lead me in a different direction. It is time to make a choice. I have encountered many such forks and know that there will be many more in the future. There will be many choices to make in life. It is my life and my path, and I must choose. It is not my mom and dad's path. It is not my friends' path or my family's path. The paths of my family members and friends run alongside mine, and we share good and bad times together. But this is my path and mine alone. It is my life. I am the one who must decide. I must make my own choice. I can ask the opinion of others but the decision is mine alone. I must choose. I must choose which path to take and then I must live with the consequences of my choice.

We face choices every day. It does not have to be a complex choice that alters the face of your entire life and state of existence. It does not have to be a divinely influenced choice that is sent down from above in a moment of complete and total clarity whereupon you are standing on a mountaintop with rays of light shining down upon you. It does not have to be a hugely momentous occasion, a crossroads that all your lifelong endeavors and pursuits have led to since the day you were born. It does not have to be what your family, spouse, children, religion, parents, or upbringing expects of you. It does not have to be something that you think long and hard about for days, months, or years until you finally arrive at it in a fantastic culmination. It does not have to be something that causes you to stand up and face harsh criticism or punishment from others. It does not cause you to feel guilt, shame, or humiliation. It does not have to be a great and worthy cause that will help end world hunger or save mother earth. It is simply a choice—great or small, tall or short, fat or skinny, life altering or infinitesimal in scale. It is a choice.

Let's return to our path. You are at the fork in the road. You are alone. This is your life and yours alone. It is you who must decide which path to follow. You look to the left and see a sunny, broad, green, and winding path. It is a happy looking little path, bright and full of adventure. You look to the right. There lies a smooth, shady, lovely, and pleasant path. It is a contented looking little path. There are easy feelings, and smooth sailing down that path. You look them over carefully, consider the possibilities and the consequences, and decide that the left path is the one for you. You have made a choice in life. Perhaps it is a big choice that may change everything or perhaps a small choice that seems to make little difference. The choice is made, and it is the path on the left. Is this an Empowering Choice or a regular, ordinary choice?

Please excuse me a moment while I indulge myself in one of my favorite pastimes—quoting songs, movies, or poems. I can't help but be reminded of what to my mind is one of the best rock lyrics of all time. As I am walking down the path and standing at the fork, having chosen a path to follow, I simply cannot help being reminded of a line from Led Zeppelin's song "Stairway to Heaven": "Yes, there are two paths you can go by, but in the long run there's still time to change the road you're on."[1] When I was in high school, each senior could choose a quote or saying to be printed beside his or her name in the yearbook. This line from "Stairway to Heaven" was a very popular one. As a high school graduate, at a time when you are going through many changes in life and the future is happening all around you, you are undoubtedly making many choices for yourself and standing at many forks in your road. In a time of great uncertainty and adjustment, how is one to make the right choice? The lyrics assure us that if we go down a particular path, and it turns out to be the wrong one, we can always go back and choose

---

[1] Led Zeppelin, "Stairway to Heaven," *Led Zeppelin IV*, 1971, Atlantic Swan Song.

the other path. You can change your mind. You are a free spirit, this is a free country, and everyone is blessed with the gift of free will. You may want to change the path that you are on for any number of reasons: you find you're not suited to the career you chose, the college you selected is overwhelming because it's so large, or what appealed to you at the onset, proves less enchanting as you learn more about it. Your priorities may change. The person that you thought you were as an adolescent, when your peers were influencing you, is no longer the person you want to be. You are having second thoughts about the religious teachings that you were raised with. You always pictured having a family early on, but now you think you want to establish your career first. You chose a path and began your journey, but now you want to change your mind. You want to go back and choose something different.

I am at the fork, and I have chosen the path on the left side. The path that is sunny, broad, green and winding. The happy looking little path. The left path is my choice. If this choice is truly an Empowering Choice, then I am absolutely, resolutely certain that it is the path for me. I am ready to defend it and work hard to achieve it, ready to face any challenges that might come my way, so that I can continue my forward movement on this path. It means so much to me that I am confident and self-assured, and I know that there will never be a need to "change the road you're on" because I have made an Empowering Choice. I am absolutely certain that the left path is the only choice for me. I am sure beyond any doubt that this is the correct decision for me in my life. That is an *Empowering Choice*. I feel empowered deep in my soul and ready to take on the world because I am convinced that I have made the right decision.

Now if it is a regular ordinary choice that is not an Empowering Choice, there will be different feelings about it. You are *trying* out the left path, you feel pretty good about it, and it looks like the correct decision for you. But you are not, however, absolutely resolutely certain of it, and you have doubts swirling around in your mind. The other path, which is smooth, shady, lovely, and pleasant, might be something you want to try if this one doesn't work out. You are not firmly committed to this course of action, so your whole heart and soul aren't engaged in the endeavor. You may want to *turn around*, *go back*, and take the other path instead at some point. That is the difference right there between an Empowering Choice and a routine choice—turning around implies regret. With an Empowering Choice, you will not ever wish to turn around and go back. You have no regrets about it. You may choose other paths, similar to the one you gave up, in the future, perhaps years down the road, but you never regret the choice you're making right here and right now.

You are a free spirit with free will, and nobody is stopping you from changing your mind, turning your little self around, and trying the other path instead sometime in the future. I know you are considering how liberating it is to know that if you are unhappy with your choice, you can change this road that you are on. This ability to change your mind about things is a wonderfully freeing and liberating feeling! What a grand thing free will is! In the words of one of my favorite rock bands, Rush (here I go again): "I will choose a path that's clear. I will choose Freewill."[2]

Free will to change your mind certainly brings with it feelings of security and contentment, knowing that you are not stuck on this path forever if it becomes unpleasant

---

[2] Rush, "Freewill," *Permanent Waves*, 1979, Mercury, Quebec.

and unlivable. Free will, however, is present in both Empowering Choices and regular choices. With Empowering Choices, you have free will to choose other things for yourself in the future. But you do not regret the choice you made before and you see it through. Perhaps you travel down the left *happy* path for some time, and you love it and do not regret your decision. But when you enter a new stage in life, you are ready to try the other path, the "road less traveled by,"[3] as poet Robert Frost termed it. For example, I will never regret my decision to become an elementary school teacher; I love teaching, but sometime in the future, I may wish to change my career and try something different. If I choose to go down a different career path in the future, it does not mean I regret the choice I made, it just means that I'm ready for something new. If this is an Empowering Choice, you will feel so confident and secure about the decision you have made that you'll never have feelings of being stuck and trapped. You know who you are, and you know what you want. While you will not regret your choice, you may, however, change your mind in the future as your stage in life changes or circumstances that are beyond your control may arise. That does not mean that you regret having chosen the left path. That Empowered Choice was the absolute right choice for you, and you do not wish to go back and take the other path instead. It just means that sometime in the future—months from now, years from now, or when I am an old lady knitting in a rocking chair—I may wish to make a change in the direction that I am going.

Let's go back to our graduating senior with all of those choices and decisions to make. All my life I was taught the

---

[3] Robert Frost, "The Road Not Taken," *Mountain Interval*, (New York: Henry Holt and Company, 1920).

value of a college degree. My parents, grandparents, and everyone around me drilled it into me. "Go to college girl, and get a degree." I had been told time and time again for as long as I can remember that getting this degree would open up doors and bring life opportunities that would be out of reach otherwise. The degree is the key. It is the answer. I made an Empowering Choice:

I will earn a college degree.

I knew that it would not be easy. I knew that the professors would not simply hand me the degree and say, "Here you go, Sara. Good luck." It would require years of diligence and hard work. There would be hours and hours of reading, extra expenses, classes, and all-nighters before tests. But I was absolutely certain that earning a college degree was the correct choice for me and that it was undeniably necessary in my life. So I set out down the path. In the middle of my senior year in high school, I went to Austin, Texas with my mother to tour the campus of the University of Texas (UT). I was enraptured. I gazed at the beautifully manicured campus, the stately old buildings, the fountains, the libraries, and the huge old oak trees in the grassy fields where college students were laying out with books in hand. I was sold. This is where I am meant to be. This is the place for me. And so we went to the admissions building. I had always been a good student, so I had no worries whatsoever that I would have a problem. I was dead wrong about that. With my class rank, my SAT score was not quite high enough. It was off, in fact by a mere one hundred points or so. Only one hundred lousy points? Come on. Don't they realize that this is fate they're messing with? I had chosen a path, and my path was the

University of Texas at Austin. The powers on high, which were entirely beyond my control, had other plans. I said to them, "Okay, there must be a way. I am coming to this school, so tell me what I have to do."

They had a program in which students just out of high school could take four courses over the summer on a provisional basis. To make the cut, I would have to earn at least a 3.25 grade point average—that is one A and three Bs. They warned me that it would be intense and difficult, and that 80 percent of the students did not make it through the program.

Two weeks after I graduated high school, I was living in a dormitory on the UT campus. Throughout the entire summer, I did not meet a single person, other than my roommate; and I did not go out socially one single time. I did not go to dinner or see a movie or hang out by a swimming pool or even shop at the mall that summer. I went to classes, and I studied from sunup to sundown. I went to test reviews, tutorials, libraries, study groups, and office hours. I was determined to make it through this program no matter what. I could not control the admissions policies of the university, but I could work my tail off and give it my best effort. At the end of the program, I had a 3.5 grade point average, two As and two Bs. I was a longhorn—Hook 'em Horns!

There are always outside forces at work that are beyond our control. Some say that life is what happens while you are making other plans. I was determined to get a college degree, and I was determined to go to the University of Texas. What if, despite my best efforts, I had been a few points short of making it through the provisional program? Plan B would have been to go to a community college for a year and then reapply. What if I had become ill and could not study so diligently that summer? What if a family emergency had interrupted my studies? What if I had a bad night and did poorly on a test that was one-half of my final grade in a course? What if my roommate turned out to be heinous and caused me so much mental anguish and despair that I could not focus on my studies? What if I got third-degree burns from lying out on the beautifully manicured campus lawns while studying? Life happens; life gets in the way. It is ever changing and unpredictable. When an Empowering Decision is made, it must be made with the realistic knowledge that life can throw curve balls. No matter what happens though, you are secure in the fact that you made a choice for yourself that was the right choice to make at the time, and you took action to fulfill it. You proceed down the path with confidence, knowing that you may not reach the summit of the mountain, but you will certainly work hard to get up there; you will forge ahead, you will enjoy the views, you will grow and learn, and you will build character. You will be a better person because you chose this path. That is enough.

An Empowering Choice is a single decision in a single moment that you make for yourself. You do not make it for the benefit of others. You make it to better your own life and your own existence. You make a decision for your body, mind, and soul. You are absolutely positive and have no doubt that it is the right choice for you. Right here and right now, at this moment in your life, it is the right choice and you are so certain of it that you will never regret the decision. You simply cannot see living your life without this decision. The decision to stick to this choice, to not waver in your conviction, to stand up for its rightness and goodness is what makes it an Empowering Choice and not an ordinary choice. Your choice allows you to live your own life free of outside opinions and influences, and makes you complete and whole onto yourself. You stand alone and apart from the whole world around you and all the people in your life. You stand for something that you have sanctioned and allowed to dominate your destiny, no matter what else the future may hold and where your path leads you. You feel hopeful for the future and that great things are in store for you. Your hard work, determination, and sound decisions meet with golden opportunities. You have made a decision to be your own advocate, to work hard for the things that you want, to seek out opportunities where none may have existed before, to be victorious in your pursuits, to be happy in your everyday life, and to make Empowering Choices that are right for you. Success is yours!

CHAPTER 3:
I RUN FOR LIFE

Early morning—the dawn of life. You open your eyes in the earliest hours with eager anticipation. This is the beginning of the journey. Every extreme emotion known to man is happening inside your soul all at once: excitement for what is to come, fear of the unknown, awe of the awesome task ahead, doubt in yourself, happiness for the potential and opportunities ahead of you, and sadness that with the beginning comes the knowledge that there will be an ending as well. The journey ahead of you is a long, winding, unpredictable road and far too mysterious for your young mind to imagine. You make your way to the start line and prepare yourself for the task ahead. 26.2 miles. The journey of life.

I am a marathon runner. I was never a natural-born athlete and do not have a speck of innate or inherent physical ability. As a child, I was lazy and avoided any activities that required excessive walking, running, biking, throwing, hitting, or sports of any kind. I did take ballet as a small child, and I enjoyed it; but when it started to get to the point that required long hours of practice and strenuous physical movements, I bailed out. When my best friend and I would go for long bike rides, I would always lag behind and call out, "Wait for me!" In physical education classes in elementary school, I could not do anything that involved hitting or catching a ball to save my life. I was always the kid chosen last for a team. And relay races or sprinting? Not a chance. In high school, it was more of the same. I dreaded having to play volleyball, baseball, or pretty much anything that involved a ball. They even tried to teach us the basics of weightlifting one time, but that was a joke. (I lift weights to strengthen twice a week regularly now.) But the absolute worst time of the school year, the one that I hated the most and would look on with anxiety and dread, was the annual one-mile run. It happened every spring, and we were required to run just one little mile, that is, only four loops around the track. It may as well have been two hundred loops. I would trudge along, pulling my feet forward step after step, shoulders hunched, head bowed, and face drawn, as the other students whizzed by me. I felt weak, embarrassed, ashamed, and genuinely humiliated. I could not run a mile. I could barely walk it.

My senior year of high school, a teacher came along and planted a seed that changed all that. It was the annual one-mile run, but this year we had to do it in less than eighteen minutes. If we couldn't go one mile in the prescribed time limit, we had to repeat it the next day and everyday thereafter until we succeeded. Well, you can imagine what happened. After four days of this, I was still at it, and I had no chance of making the run in the time limit. I was miserable and exhausted, and this was more exercise than I had probably had in my life. Was the teacher encouraging? Did she offer advice and words of support and motivation? The teacher told me, "Don't worry about it, Sara. I'll let you off for this one. *I don't think you have it in you to be a runner anyway."*

She actually said that to me. I don't have it in me to be a runner. I changed that day. A fire was lit inside of me. The words she had said repeated in my mind over and over and over again. I don't have it in me to be a runner. The words tumbled through my mind—I do not have it in me. I don't have what it takes. I remembered how I felt being the last one off the track while the other students were already halfway to the lockers. I thought of how I felt being the only one still out there after four days because everyone else had made the time limit except me. I was humiliated and ashamed. I told myself that this was just how it was for me; this was the hand I was dealt. The other students are athletic, and I am not. Was this the person I wanted to be? Did I want to always be the last one to finish, just scraping by as best I can, trudging along with shoulders down and head bowed? Do I want to feel sorry for myself and just accept that I don't have it in me? Do I want to believe that this is just who I am, and there is nothing I can do about it? Do I even have a choice or was this path already chosen for me?

There was a choice and I made it—an Empowering Choice. I was not going to be the kind of person who accepts her limits and boundaries, and settles for less. I was not going to be the kind of person who gives up and accepts the status quo. I was not going to plod along and let other people or circumstances make choices for me. I was not going to be told that I don't have it in me to be a runner or to be anything else that I want to be. I decided that I would start believing in myself, and decide what I wanted and work as hard as I could to achieve it. I would not sit back and wait for my dreams to fall in my lap, but I was going to go out and chase after them. Perhaps I would even find new dreams to chase and new rainbows that I hadn't even considered because they seemed impossible and beyond my reach. I would keep pushing on even when it became so hard and my hope was almost gone. I would be a determined, passionate, stubborn, strong, proud, independent person. I will have my shoulders back and my head up. I will push myself through any boundaries and limitations, and I will break through them.

I will be a runner.

And so I got some cute little running clothes, a sturdy pair of running shoes, a very supportive running bra, and a rather expensive gym membership. I walked into the gym and looked around me. "Look at all these people!" I said to myself. "Do I really belong here? Don't worry about it. Just don't look them in the eye and get on the treadmill." I got on the treadmill and hit the start button. I got the speed up to a slow jogging pace. I was on my way! How long did I last until I was tired out and ready to slow down? Exactly thirty seconds.

But I was not discouraged. I was armed with the lyrics of one of my favorite rock bands of all time, REO Speedwagon: "You may not know this but you are everything you've ever needed."[1] I repeated the words in my head over and over. Everyone has to start somewhere. I may not have stamina or muscle tone yet, but I do have a stubborn iron will. So I returned to the gym each day and did an interval of running and walking. I would run for thirty seconds and walk for ten minutes, and I repeated this three or four times each session. After several weeks of that, I could run for one minute and walk for nine minutes. I slowly increased my running time and decreased the walking time. I began to see that I needed fewer walking breaks and was able to run for longer and longer periods. I could control my breathing and get into a comfortable stride and rhythm. The minutes spent running were not exactly pleasant or fun, but I was making progress. I continued this routine for about a year or so.

---

[1] REO Speedwagon, "Only the Strong Survive," *The Essential REO Speedwagon*, 1979, Sony Music Entertainment, Inc.

In 2001, I ran my first 5k. I will never forget the feeling. I was a runner. There I was standing at the start line with hundreds of other runners, and I had a bib pinned to my shirt with my very own race number. Dawn was just breaking, we sang the national anthem, the loud shot rang out, and everyone took off. I made my away around the winding streets of Austin, taking in all of the sights and sounds. The spectators lined the streets and cheered us on. Crossing the finish line felt amazing, but as it turned out, it was actually more of a *start* line for future races to come. After the race someone handed me a flyer for a 10K. "Why not?" I said to myself.

More 5k races were to follow, each one more gratifying and reaffirming than the last. Then in 2003, some of my friends told me they were doing a 10K. I had never run further than three miles. Did I have it in me? Could I run 6.1 miles? I remembered my Empowering Choice and the words that the teacher had said. I made a promise to myself to push my boundaries and my limits, and to be all I was capable of being. I signed up for the race. I stood at another start line in downtown Austin. It was raining, and I was afraid of the road being slippery and the hilly terrain. The first four miles came easy, but the last two were difficult. I was exhausted that last mile and had to use every once of mental energy. Then I rounded the corner, and I saw the huge finish line and the spectators cheering for me. I ran a 10K.

I was beginning to see that each finish line was not merely a destination, but actually another starting point. If I can run a 10K, why couldn't I push myself even further? I had learned that even though I had not been born with a natural talent or ability to run, it was something I could do through hard work, determination, and mental stamina.

The fact that it did not come easy for me made it all the more gratifying. The way I saw myself and the way I saw the world was changing. Walls that had always been there were crumbling. I believed in myself. Things that were not possible before were now within reach because *I had made an Empowering Choice*.

In 2003 I registered for a half- marathon and a training program. The first day I went out to run with the group in the training program, I couldn't help but think, "What am I doing out here? I am not like these people. These are long-distance runners and athletes. Am I an athlete?" Yet every week I would show up early Saturday morning, and the mileage I ran would get longer and longer. The feeling of training for and completing that first half marathon cannot be described. In March 2004, I made the following entry in my running journal:

> On January 18, 2004, I completed my first half marathon in Houston, Texas. I ran the whole way and felt great, except for those small but mighty blisters on my pinky toes. It was quite a journey getting there—years in the making, really. But I see now that it wasn't an end in itself but only a step along the way. Two hours and eighteen minutes (give or take). It was, in a way, an affirmation of my character. I am stubborn and relentless. Determined and fierce about what I want. I pushed my own limitations and stretched them as far as I could. I ran a half marathon. Nobody can take that away from me. And when something gets hard in life, I only have to look at that medal and remember where I started and how far I went. How I changed my life. How I went after my dreams, as hard as every step toward them was. And the feeling inside when I

crossed the finish line—I can do anything! And now I'm ready for the whole marathon. I know now that I can do it. I know there will be many bumps in the road, dark streets, sneakers that leak, and pain! But I've got the eye of the tiger. It's the moment of truth. How far can you push your boundaries? When I can't run another step, I'll keep pushing to the finish.

How could this be? Was I the same person as that slope-shouldered, insecure, lazy girl in high school who could not run one mile in gym class? The same one the teacher said didn't have it in her to be a runner? How did I get from there to here? I made an Empowering Choice. I chose a path. I decided to be the person I dreamed of being. I decided to be strong and capable, and to be proud of myself. I am going to do the impossible. I registered for the 2005 Houston Marathon and a six-month marathon-training program.

The six months of training were grueling, time consuming, life changing, awe inspiring, brutal, and extremely intense. I ran three to six miles several times a week. I met my running group at the park each Saturday at insanely early hours of the morning. On our first four-mile run, I was thinking that it was so hard, and I didn't know how I would go further the following week. Next week came, and I ran five miles and wondered how I would possibly run six the next week. This happened week after week with eight-mile runs, then ten-mile runs, then twelve-mile runs, and on and on. I read running books. I ate nutritiously. I ran for hours and hours and hours. I sweated, stretched, and iced my knees. I got ingrown toenails! And I met awesome, inspiring runners who became my good friends. I became part of the running community. I was becoming a distance runner and an athlete before my very eyes. I could write an entire book about all the events that transpired in those six months. But suffice it to say that I knew all that hard work, blood, sweat, and tears would pay off in the end.

On Saturday, November 27, 2004, I made the following entry in my running journal:

I ran 19 miles today.
I am able to leap tall buildings in a single bound.
Three hours and forty-five minutes.
I am still alive to tell the tale.
This guy fell and skinned his knee around mile six. There was a rest stop at mile eleven with the best PB&J sandwiches I ever had. Krista hurt her IT band[2] and couldn't finish. I ran with Amy and Christie. I felt pretty good.

I had somehow pushed my threshold further then I ever thought possible. I gathered up my strength, and told myself that I was strong and capable and that I could do anything I set my mind too. I told myself that the only boundaries were the ones I created for myself. On Sunday, December 19, 2004, I made the following entry in my running journal:

The marathon is four weeks from today. Yesterday was my peak training run—22 miles. It took longer than I wanted it to—four hours and forty-five minutes, but it was on trails, and I stopped at a restroom twice. Several rest and stretch breaks too. I felt a surge toward the end—a second wind. All in all, it was a positive

---

[2] Illiotibial band syndrome is a common injury with runners and is characterized by discomfort or pain in the tissue on the outside of the thigh, between the knee and the hip.

experience, and I am encouraged for the marathon. I know I can do it!

On January 15, 2005, I made the following entry in my running journal:

Tomorrow is my marathon. That's funny—six thousand people are running it, but it's *MY* marathon. Feeling excited. Butterflies in tummy. A little nervous. I've put in my time, and all the hard work will pay off tomorrow. I will make it to the finish. I'm going to treat it like every other training run, and I'm going to think of it that way. Every mile will be worth my while.

On January 16, 2005, I ran the Houston Marathon. I ran 26.2 miles. It took me five hours, twenty-nine minutes, and forty-six seconds. I ran it for me. According to marathon-runner and author John "the Penguin" Bingham, as a long-distance athlete, I was now fitter, better trained, and more disciplined than 99 percent of the population *that has ever lived*.[3] I was in one tenth of 1 percent of the world's population. ME! An athlete, a long-distance runner, and a marathon finisher. Unbelievable.

Some runners finish their first marathon and tell themselves that it was a great experience and wonderful accomplishment but it was also grueling and punishing and they vow never to do it again. Not me. I couldn't wait to start my next one. Just to prove to myself that the first time wasn't a total fluke, I ran the Houston Marathon again in January 2006. It turns out that training for and running your second marathon is just as difficult and time consuming as the first time around. The first marathon is unknown

---

[3] Bingham, John, and Jenny Hadfield. *Marathoning for Mortals*. Emmaus, Pa.: Rodale Books, 2003.

and romanticized. The runner simply has no idea what they are in for. The second marathon comes with blessed memories of sore muscles, aching knees, upset tummies, chafed skin, the post-marathon staggering walk, not being able to step down from the curb or sit down on the toilet, and knowing you have miles to go when every fiber of your being wants you to stop. The amazing feeling you get from crossing the finish line makes the journey worth it, and I knew that because I had done it already. Then, at our post race celebration, I was talking amongst my running buddies, and they were all sporting their finest shiny medals around their necks when I spotted a medal shaped like the head of Mickey Mouse. A Mickey medal? A Walt Disney World Marathon that runs 26.2 miles through the happiest place on earth? Where do I sign up?

For the third time, I went through six long months of marathon training. As I said, the six months are grueling, but they are also invigorating and, clearly, addicting. Getting up at four o'clock in the morning every Saturday becomes a way of life, and when it's all over, it is difficult to imagine life without it. My motto for the Disney World Marathon came from a Disney song called "Remember the Magic": "The secret of tomorrow is to live your dreams today."[4]

In January 2007, I went to Orlando, Florida, with my best friend, Carla. We had a great time touring the park in the days before the marathon and rode all the rides, wore matching pirate hats with big Mickey ears, and had plenty of big Mickey-shaped ice creams. However, I do not recommend walking miles and miles around Walt Disney

---

[4] Brian McKnight, "Remember the Magic," *Disney's Greatest Pop Hits*, 1996, Wonderland Music Company.

World before running a marathon. I woke up on marathon morning at 2:30 A.M.! It was very hot and muggy outside, and it felt like I was standing in the middle of a swamp. Far from ideal weather for the task I was undertaking. In my running journal I wrote:

> Mickey and the gang were all there, and there were fireworks at the start line. Most of the race was between the parks, and it was hotter than the surface of the sun. There was entertainment, bands, music, and tons of people. I took lots of pictures with characters in the parks. It was awesome running through the parks. After the first half, most people were walking from the heat. It was very difficult, but I drank lots of water and walked when I needed to; I was determined to finish and not get heat exhaustion. Many people passed out or got sick and didn't finish. People crossed the finish line and promptly threw up or passed out. At mile 20 I reached a turning point. I saw a lady struggling, and then she just suddenly stopped, lowered herself to the curb, and slouched over in total defeat. You could see it in the look on her face and her body language. She was done. At that point I said to myself that is *NOT* going to be me.

The circumstances in my third marathon made it much more difficult than the first two. It was the best of times, and the worst of times. Walt Disney himself said, "It's kind of fun to do the impossible."[5] Life is unpredictable, and no matter how much you prepare for something, life happens, and the big day is not guaranteed to be picture perfect. But I wanted that medal, and I was willing to pay the price

---

[5] Walt Disney, US Cartoonist and Movie Producer, 1901-1966.

to get it. The price was to finish the 26. 2 miles no matter what curve balls were thrown at me. I wanted to run up Main Street and through Cinderella's castle, around World Showcase, past Spaceship Earth, and under Mickey's sorcerer's hat while snapping pictures with all of the characters. I got my medal, and it's my prized possession. Disney really is where dreams come true.

My marathons taught me so many life lessons and much about myself. They changed me profoundly and helped mold me into the person I wanted to be and the person I am today. I knew that anything was possible. Anything I ever wanted in life was achievable with effort and hard work. It was that high school teacher that started me down this road, and I have her to thank. I don't have it in me to be a runner? I'll take that apology now.

CHAPTER 4:
I DREAMED A DREAM OF RUNNING

I love to run. When I am jogging along at a comfortable pace around the three-mile track at Rice University or the loop at Memorial Park, under the shade of the beautiful trees, in the humidity and scorching heat of a lovely Houston day, I am at peace with the world. The trees are green, the path is welcoming, and I have the air in my lungs and a strong healthy body. Sometimes it is uncomfortable—there can be aches, tightness, and pain. But that's okay because a little pain lets you know that you are alive. It's more gratifying with pain. Tasks that are difficult to bear are sweet to remember. If it were easy, everyone would do it. I am on a solitary run under a blue sky. I am where I belong. I am where I am supposed to be. My mind is clear, and I have no thoughts, no problems, no worries, and no responsibilities. Nothing is required of me but to put one foot in front of the other. All I have is the path that lays ahead and the peaceful rhythm of my steps. And just for that moment, it is all I need. It is enough, and I am humbled.

In 2007, I set my sights on a new running goal. I began training for the Marine Corps Marathon in Washington, DC. I had been to the Washington, DC area before, and having a love for American history, I immediately fell in love with the city. I loved the museums, the National Archives, the stately buildings, the U.S. Capitol, and especially the memorials. I was awed by the statue of Lincoln sitting on his thrown, seemingly deep in thought, in his memorial, the star spangled banner which inspired our national anthem, the rows of white headstones at Arlington Cemetery, and the rotunda on Capitol hill atop which Liberty herself stands. So when I heard that there was a marathon that curved 26.2 miles around all these amazing sights, I was sold. Just tell me where to sign.

The finish line of the Marine Corps Marathon is in Arlington Cemetery at the Marine Corps Memorial Statue. The statue depicts six marines raising an American flag on Iwo Jima in World War II. A Pulitzer prize-winning photograph taken by Joe Rosenthal that is the most reproduced photograph of all time inspired the statue. So I began training for what would be my fourth marathon.

As I was training, I decided that my triumphant finish would be all the more meaningful if I knew a little something about that statue. I made it a quest. As you may have realized by this point, I tend to obsess and go overboard. Who were the six men? Where were they from? How old were they? Why were they raising that flag? How did Rosenthal happen to take the picture? Who built the amazing statue and how did they build it? What was the battle of Iwo Jima all about? Why was America in the Pacific fighting Japan in the first place? I had to find the answers, and I had to know the names of the men, their life stories, and what became of them. I started with the book *Flags of Our Fathers* by James Bradley, son of flag raiser John Bradley. It was an amazing book, and after reading it twice, I was completely hooked on the history of the Pacific War and Iwo Jima. I read every book I could get my hands on. I watched television programs, documentaries, and movies on the subject. I got a huge poster of the flag-raising photograph and hung it in my bedroom, so I would see it when I woke up every morning. My family thought I was completely nuts and had fallen off the deep end.

My new obsession with Iwo Jima, the flag raising statue, and Pacific War history took on a life of its own. But it was also inextricably connected with the Marine Corps Marathon. My love of the flag-raising photograph made the goal of the marathon all the more meaningful and special to me. The flag raisers were courageous, determined, selfless, and brave. They were heroes, although they themselves would have argued that point. They hated being called heroes and contended that the men who fought and died on the island were the real heroes (although three of the six flag raisers did just that). They raised that flag, so that I could be free. If I could run the Marine Corps Marathon, it would not just be for me, it would also be to honor them. Indeed, to honor those six marines specifically, but also all marines, past and present, who put their life on the line for love of their country and freedom for all. This marathon became something much more than the other three. I had run the other three just for me, but now I was running it in honor, reverence, and respect for all members of the Marine Corps.

Trouble began four months into the training; my right calf was the first to speak up and complain. It decided it had quite enough of this abuse, overuse, and tomfoolery. That was all it could stand, and it could not take any more. The right calf staged a protest. It picketed in the streets and held up signs saying, "Good grief, woman, give us a rest!" It talked other muscles into joining its cause. Soon the hamstring, the lower back, the hip, and the gluteus had joined the battle.

"Come on now, guys," the muscles of my left side told their counterparts on the right. "Let's cooperate with her. It's really not so bad. She is making us strong! That which doesn't kill you makes you stronger!"

The right muscles would have none of it, especially the gluteus. The gluteus had some very angry creatures in it. The angry creatures got the ultimate revenge, for they were in a perfect position to wreak all kinds of havoc. You see they had a lovely little nerve, called the sciatic, which runs right past them and all the way down to the toe. So the gluteus thought, "Hmmm, I know! I'll just pinch on this nerve a little bit, and her foot will be numb and tingly! Then she won't be able to run, and maybe we can all get a little rest! While I'm at it, I'll just send a little referred pain up to her lower back and really put her on the sidelines!"

In September of 2007, six weeks before the marathon, I went to Philadelphia, Pennsylvania, to run a half marathon. I just barely made it to the finish line. I was able to make it only with the support of a running buddy and the enticement of a medal in the shape of the liberty bell. As I sat in the airport with pain in my back and a numb foot, I knew my Marine Corps Marathon plans were history. I was brokenhearted.

On September 16, 2007, I made the following entry in my running journal:

> Okay. So, either you run, feel great, and finish, or you postpone until next year. Starting and not finishing is not an option. If you decide not to, it's not quitting or failing. It's simply a postponement until next year, when your back is well rested and 100 percent healed. You do not give up on what you want. You get what you want. It may take longer than you planned, but you will see Iwo Jima at the finish, and you will wear that medal forever and ever. I pledge, and I promise, and I absolutely swear it on my life. Whether it happens in 2007 or 2020, I don't care. But it will. So help me.

I made an Empowering Choice. It was a choice to continue to be a runner. It was a choice to do everything in my power and in my control to make my dream come true. But it was more than that—it was a choice to be the kind of person who does not give up, even in the face of great obstacles. I will have fortitude, just as my flag raisers did. I will confront fear, pain, uncertainty, and intimidation.
I will not give up.

I was an injured runner, and for the next nine months, I searched for an answer, leaving no stone unturned. The first thing I did was get an MRI that showed that I had a tiny, little bitty disc bulge in my back, but it was so small that it was unlikely to be causing my problem. Doctor number one, a sports-medicine specialist, gave me all kinds of anti-inflammatory medications and steroids, and sent me to two different physical therapy clinics. The numbness and tingling in my foot eased up a bit, but as soon as I started exercising again, it came right back. Doctor number two, my regular internist, did an MRI of my head and neck to make sure I didn't have any nasty diseases that could cause all this. Doctor number three, an orthopedist, did not help me whatsoever. Doctor number four, a chiropractor, did adjustments several times a week for several months. That helped at first, but the symptoms returned and got so bad that I could barely walk or fall asleep. I tried acupuncture at that point, but I was unconvinced that it was going to solve my underlying problem. Doctor number five, a neurologist, prescribed steroids and muscle relaxers. The muscle relaxers helped, so the doctor diagnosed that the problem was obviously muscular. It took five doctors to come up with that brilliant conclusion. My next treatment came from a massage therapist who did deep tissue massages a few times a week for several months. At first I thought I was getting somewhere with the massages, but then my pain, numbness, and tingling returned and was worse than ever. I stopped taking the muscle relaxers. Doctors six and seven, pain-management specialists, said they could not do anything for me because my pain was so varied and widespread.

After nine months of this, I had been to an internist, an orthopedist, a neurologist, pain management specialists, a chiropractor, massage therapists, physical therapists, and sports medicine specialists. All the while, I could not run or exercise whatsoever; my back ached, my right foot was numb and tingly as I lay in bed at night, and my light bulb of hope that had been burning bright was beginning to fade. I was pretty grumpy and pessimistic all the time too, so you didn't want to get on my bad side. I made the following entry in my running injury journal:

> The referred pain is down the back of the leg, and there is numbness in right foot and big toe. The tight glutes sound like trigger points, but sometimes my SI joint[1] in my low back kills also. I can't exercise whatsoever, or it gets really fired up. Some days I feel fine, some days left SI joint kills, some days right buttock kills, and some days the whole butt just kills. Some days right hamstring, right calf, right foot, and lower back or even middle back hurts! It varies so much! And I can't do cardio at all or it'll be totally fired up. Poor me! I'm in pain and discomfort everyday.

---
[1] The sacroiliac joint is in the low back on either side of the spine.

I had been to doctor after doctor. I had taken medication after medication. I had taken a million different kinds of anti-inflammatory, enough ibuprofen to supply a small country, and anything else that the doctors recommended. Nothing helped. Sometimes it helped briefly for a short period of time, but after several days or weeks, the pain and numbness would return. If I could just run, I would be happy. If my foot would stop tingling, I would be happy. If my back would stop hurting, I would be happy. If I could just walk up my block, I would be happy. I would drive past the park and see the other runners flying along effortlessly, and I would wonder if they knew how lucky they were. Perhaps it's true that everything happens for a reason. One thing I knew for certain—I would never again take running for granted. I would never complain about having to go for a run; having to get up at 5:00 A.M. on a Saturday to meet my group; having to run in the humidity, rain, heat, or cold; or having to go to the gym after work to exercise. I knew for certain that I would never regret becoming a runner and running my marathons. Even with all of this turmoil and pain, having to chase after doctors and diagnoses, I would never regret it. I had made an Empowering Choice, and I did not feel regret.

In May 2008, I was nearing the end of my rope. I was climbing an uphill battle, unable to run even a single block, and I was hanging on to hope by a very thin thread. I walked into the office of Dr. Ed Kieke, doctor number eight; he is the founder and CEO of Koala Health and Wellness Center, Inc., a chiropractic and physical therapy clinic geared specifically toward athletes and runners. I had already been to another chiropractor and I had been to two physical therapy clinics. I had no reason to believe or hope that this would be any different than all of the rest. Nonetheless, there I was. I handed him my detailed history, which specified all the doctors, treatments, and medications I had tried.

"I don't think you can help me," I said. "I've tried everything. Running means so much to me, but I just can't run anymore."

He told me that he could help me and that I should trust him. He explained how he would use a combination of treatments and rehabilitation that would have me on my feet and running again. He smiled and said this with complete confidence and assurance. I left his office, bought a boatload of licorice and chocolate to console myself, and sat in my car and cried. How could I find the strength to keep fighting this fight? I would invest more money, time, and effort and be no better off. I had already invested so much in this pursuit that each disappointment had beat me to the ground more and more. But in the end I figured I had nothing more to lose, so I decided to give Dr. Kieke's plan a try.

I went to Koala three times a week for the next year. This was not easy because I had to drive to downtown Houston, park in the costly garage, and take the elevator up to the forty-second floor. Once school started, the trek became even more difficult as I battled rush-hour traffic; I also had to hire a dog walker to take care of my pooch's needs. When he saw me, Dr. Kieke (Dr. K) would put a great big grin on his face, give me a big pat on the back, and say, "Smile!" I had not really smiled in a long time. I would give him a half-hearted smile that we both knew was a fake. But I kept going and clung desperately to the thin thread of hope that I would run again. I worked very hard everyday, stretching, icing, heating, and strengthening with weights. I got electrolysis therapy and especially liked the little buzzers zapping against the pain like sweet little butterflies taking it away. I had bruises along my legs, hips, and back from the deep-tissue massages, although the therapists would joke that the Koala's had bitten me. I began to spend long hours at the gym doing the weight routine that the Koala therapists had shown me, in addition to going downtown for therapy and deep-tissue massages each week. I took Epsom salt baths each night, and Koala became my home away from home. I continued day after day, week after week, and month after month until a whole year had flown by.

In May 2009, two years after first training to run the marathon, I began to train *again* for the Marine Corps Marathon.

Almost one year since my first visit to Dr. K, when I had proclaimed that he couldn't help me, the good Doc was celebrating a significant birthday. On that birthday I went out to the park and ran six miles. *Unbelievable.* How could I ever thank him? I was lying in bed in the middle of the night wondering how I could show him my gratitude on his birthday when a poem appeared in my head. I jumped out of bed like I was on a spring, grabbed a pen and paper, and wrote it down with passion and fury. The poem is now posted in Dr. K's office so patients see it as they first walk in. I wanted the other patients to know that if they stick with it and don't give up, they will find their smile just like I did. Not a fake smile, but a real one from the heart. I wrote this poem in May 2009 for a doctor who became my hero. He helped me to rediscover my dream, and he helped me find my smile.

I dreamed a dream of running
I dreamed it through and through
I searched for it each afternoon
Each day and evening too
Although the sky grew darker
With shades of misty blue
I would not give up searching
For I remembered and I knew
That running was inside my heart
And could not be removed
So I searched and searched
And with the dawn…I found it
And I thank you

I am not sorry for taking this dark and difficult path, for it taught me a lesson that I could only learn by going through it:
Never give up.

One of my favorite movie series of all time is the Rocky series with Sylvester Stallone. In the sixth installment, a movie titled *Rocky Balboa*, Rocky gives a speech to his son:
"You, or me, or nobody is gonna hit as hard as life. But it ain't about how hard you hit. It's about how hard you can get hit and keep moving forward—how much you can take and keep moving forward. That's how winning is done. Now if you know what your worth, go out and get what your worth. But you got to be willing to take the hits."[2]

---

[2] *Rocky Balboa*, Film. Directed by Sylvestor Stallone. Culver City, CA: Sony Pictures, 2006.

After I saw that scene, I kept rewinding it and replaying it over and over again. It is such a powerful scene and such powerful words. It takes real courage to walk through a storm and to keep going. Life is unpredictable, and sometimes it is unfair and unforgiving. Often, it makes choices for us that are the last choices we would ever make for ourselves. That is life. You can accept the circumstances that lie before you or you can choose to be *Empowered*. You can choose to move forward. You may not actually be able to touch the sky, but it won't matter because you chose to not give up. You are a winner no matter what because you didn't make excuses or apologies, and you kept going. I have been blessed with a good family, a good upbringing, and opportunities in life. I know that there are people out there who struggle with circumstances that are far worse than anything I have ever been through or ever will have to go through. I am grateful for my opportunities, and I am sorry for those who are less fortunate. But I truly believe that anyone can rise above circumstances, addictions, and obstacles to achieve greatness. You achieve greatness by reaching for it and not giving up. That is how you win at this game of life. It's not about actually achieving your dreams; it's about reaching for them and not giving up when things start to get too hard.

My second six months of training for the Marine Corps Marathon in 2009 was less than ideal. I had setbacks and continued to go to Koala for help. There was much more required of me than the other times I had trained to prevent a reoccurrence of my injury. At one point, I was doing much of my mileage aqua jogging in a swimming pool, and I spent a lot of time with weights, stretching, icing, heating, and continued therapy at Koala, driving downtown several times a week in addition to my work-out schedule.

Beating the Bridge

On October 25, 2009, I went to Washington, DC, and I ran the Marine Corps Marathon. Unlike my other marathons, I was not convinced on race day that I would actually finish, but I was determined to give it my best shot. I told myself that it didn't matter if I got to the finish line because getting to the start line was triumph enough. There is a bridge at mile 20 of the marathon, and runners have to reach that bridge at a certain time—it's referred to as *beating the bridge*. It's the way of the Marine Corps to take something that's extremely difficult and throw a monkey wrench in to make it even more difficult. If you do not reach the bridge in time, you are not allowed to finish. They put you on a bus, drive you to the finish, and you do not get your medal. As I stood at the start line, I envisioned the bridge—my final obstacle in this fight, which I had spent every moment of my spare time working toward for over two years. I thought about that bridge every minute, every hour, and every mile of that race. Would I reach it in time? Would I reach it *at all*? I reached that bridge with eight minutes to spare. In a way, crossing the bridge was the biggest moment of the marathon for me, perhaps even bigger than the actual finish line, because it was at that moment that I absolutely knew that I overcame this long, painful journey. I made the following entry in my journal that day:

> Finally I passed by a mile marker sign that said Mile 26 and I knew that I would see my statue in a minute. We turned a corner, and there was a short, steep hill in front of us. Along both sides of the road the Marines in fatigues lined up, shouting at us and holding out their hands for us to slap as we passed by. I decided not to walk but to run up that hill and I slapped

all of their hands. At the top, I turned the corner, and the final stretch lay before me. There were red arches that said Marine Corps Finish Line; I saw my image on a big screen TV and waved. Then, at long last, I crossed under the arch, and I was finished. A marine lieutenant placed my medal around my neck. I saw my statue and my flag raisers, larger than life. The lieutenant said, "Congratulations, ma'am," and I said, "Thank you very much, sir. I did it."

So that is the end of my story—a glorious triumphant ending. The perfect weather, beautiful course, handsome marines, my nation's capital, my flag raisers statue, and a medal with an eagle and an anchor—what could be better? A perfect day.

It was everything I had hoped for and more. All the stars aligned, and everything fell into place. All my hard work during the past two and a half years culminated in a glorious moment and a fantastic day. I think that I was all I was capable of being, and more, realizing my full potential, and exceeding it. All there is left to say is: Earned. Never Given.

Earned. Never Given. That is the motto of the United States Marine Corps. If you want something bad enough, you have to be willing to work for it and do whatever it takes. You have to *earn* it. It will not be handed to you on a silver platter, and it may not always be a bed of roses. But giving up is not an option. If you know it's the right path for you, then you will stick with it. Even if I had not completed the marathon, I would have counted myself a winner. I am a winner because I had the courage to start this journey, the perseverance to continue, and the sheer stubbornness not to give up. As a Marine would say "Oorah!"

G R. Irwin, MD ran the Marine Corps Marathon in 1983 in honor of his second cousin who was killed on Iwo Jima during World War II. He wrote a poem about his run that ends:

"Today I did not finish first nor last, but I gave as much as I would endure. And somehow among all these symbols of dreams and promises, I finished the course and shed a tear of happiness. For the pain I felt seemed nothing now, for I have shared in a small way today, the struggle of all these dreams and sacrifices."[3]

---

[3] Banker, George. "Introduction." In *The Marine Corps Marathon: A Running Tradition*. illustrated edition ed. Oxford: Meyer & Meyer Fachverlag Und Buchhandel Gmbh, 2007.

CHAPTER 5: HALF A SOUL

There is a Jewish tradition that tells us that God created each soul at the beginning of time, and He split each soul in half. As each soul goes through life, its purpose is to meet the other half that will make them complete. When you meet your other half, you will be complemented in every way, and you will then be a whole person. When I was growing up, my mom would tell me this story. I believed that fate or divine intervention would lead me to my other half. I believed that when I found my other half, I would know it as surely as I know the sun will shine. I think that at some point we all want to believe that there is a predetermined path for each of us, a path that has already been chosen for us at birth, and no matter what choices we make for ourselves, we will inevitably find that path. It sure is a romantic notion and a lovely thought. Maybe it is true and maybe it's not. I don't know what I believe where that is concerned and I don't think I have to decide that just yet or maybe ever. Either way, I still have my free will, so I will continue on down the road and hope for the best.

When I was in my twenties, I looked around me and realized that I had not found my other half yet. I was certain that by that time in my life, I would have found him. I had dates and romantic interests that came and went, but the plans I had made for a husband and a family were not happening as I had expected. My friends were finding their mates and getting married—I had a closet full of bridesmaid dresses to prove it. What was going on with my life? What direction was I headed in? I could go on thousands of dates, and I probably have by now, but it seemed that finding my other half was rather like finding a needle in a haystack. How would I possibly find him? Then I realized that I felt like half a person—half a soul waiting for my other half. If I never found him or if I lost him, I would have to be half a soul forever. It was ridiculous. I didn't want to be just a half. I didn't want to feel incomplete. It was not about finding romance, finding a soul mate, getting married, or living happily ever after. That would come or not, and I can only exert so much control and influence over that. You can't choose to find love. I can choose to put myself out there, take chances with people, have an open mind, accept blind dates, go to parties, go online, and have a date every day of the week. But in the end, it will happen or it won't. It is inconsequential.

I did not want to be half a soul, and I did not want to see myself that way. Even if I chose to believe that there was somebody for me out there, I could not believe that I was born with half a soul and had been living that way my entire life. Surely there must be a whole soul inside of me. I wanted to be emotionally independent and have self-awareness and confidence. I wanted to look inside myself and know with certainty who I am, accept my flaws and shortcomings, and forgive myself for them. I wanted to identify my characteristics that I liked, as well as those I disliked. I wanted to make positive efforts to change what I disliked about myself, so that I could move forward down my path with self-respect. I did not want to rely on others for approval, attention, or support. I wanted my friends, family, and loved ones to walk beside me with loyalty and trust, and to be there if I should need an ear, a shoulder, or a helping hand. But I knew that this was my path, and mine alone, and when or if I found my significant other, his path would either go alongside mine or perhaps overlap mine, but I would maintain my own character, my own interests, and my own whole, complete soul.

I now had a quest. Discover who I am and raise my self-awareness, so that I feel like a whole entire soul and not a half. My first order of business was to get a journal and use it to explore my thoughts more deeply. I went to the bookstore and looked at the blank-book section. One of the blank books had a quote from artist and author Flavia Weedn: "My Favorite old car had no reverse gear. It taught me I could only go forward."[1] Perfect! This fit right into my philosophy of moving forward down your path, and remembering and learning from the past. Never forget where you came from but do not linger there day and night, dwelling on it—face forward and move forward.

I brought my new journal home and got started. The first thing I did was print out a picture of the Iwo Jima flag raising photograph and paste it inside. Underneath the picture I wrote the words that are engraved on the bronze statue in Arlington Cemetery: *Uncommon Valor was a Common Virtue*. The photograph and the statue depicting the six marines raising the flag in World War II had come to symbolize perserverence and fortitude in my life. It reminded me that with strength and courage, one could overcome and achieve greatness.

I wrote several more quotations in my journal from my favorite rockers, motivational movies, and inspiring poets. I actually have books and books of quotations, lyrics, and poetry that I have collected through the years. I have read them so frequently that I have most of them memorized; I love to bore others by reciting them on long road trips or

---

[1] Flavia Weedn. *My Favorite Old Car Had No Reverse Gear. It Taught Me I Could Only Go Forward.* Cedco Publishing Company, 2004.

long runs. The purpose of this journal was not to collect favorite quotations, however. It was to explore who I was. So I wrote a list of things I liked about myself. It was actually more difficult than I thought it would be to compose this list! Some of the characteristics included intelligent, not ugly (don't you love that one?), driven, dedicated, passionately obsessive, hard working but sometimes lazy, loyal, caring, creative, and patient (sometimes). It was not quite a list that exudes enormous self-confidence, but it was a start. To balance that list, I made a list of things I do not like about myself, including I'm boring, I don't like my body (what girl does?), I have negative thoughts and feelings sometimes, I don't feel comfortable in a crowd of people at a party or bar, I'm sometimes quiet and withdrawn which is interpreted as being stuck-up, and I do not feel sexy or desirable. It took a lot of guts to actually write these things about myself down on paper in permanent ink and look at them in black and white. It made it real, somehow—I was owning it. The upside was that these were all characteristics that were either being misinterpreted by my negatively slanted view of myself, or they were things that I could work on and change.

More lists followed. I listed the things for which I am grateful, the things that I want, things that are preventing me from getting what I want, and negative thoughts and beliefs. I made a chart of things I want to change about myself and listed ways that I could translate that desire for change into action. For example, I said that I was uncomfortable sometimes in a crowd of people, so I enlisted the help of my girlfriends. I told them I was trying to be more outgoing and talkative with people in a crowd that I had just met or didn't know very well. We went out to bars and parties several times a week for a month or so. I made a conscious effort to approach people, begin conversations, respond appropriately and casually, and ask questions that initiated discussion. In one particular journal entry I wrote:

> I went out on Friday and Saturday night. I had a good time, and my friend Jenny said I was being sociable last night with lots of people around. It felt great. I liked being around people, and I felt like last night I made a big step.

I was moving forward in a positive direction, embracing what I liked about myself, and making specific efforts to change what I didn't like. Over several years, I made more lists and entries in my journal. I listed specific goals to meet and ways to change things about myself. I wrote about life, love, and about my frustrations with the running injury. On a day when I was feeling particularly down and pessimistic about my dating situation I made the following entry:

> First guys used me. Then I decided I deserve to be treated well, so I have 1,001 first dates. I like him, so he doesn't like me. He likes me, but I don't like him. I take a chance, and I still get screwed. All of my friends seeming to effortlessly have prince charming knock on their door and say, "Hi! Let's have a baby!" You're damned if you do, and you're damned if you don't. I say that maybe it'll be different this time. Remember, I am a three-time marathon finisher.[2] We aren't easily discouraged, and we never give up. But there are only so many walls you can hit. There's just only so much you can take. My Weight Watcher leader said, *"You*

---

[2] At the time of the journal entry, I had run not yet completed my fourth marathon.

don't always get what you deserve when you deserve it." Well, I'm trying to be patient. That's all I can do. I've got no choice. But it sure does suck being me sometimes. There. That's how I feel today. So you can take your optimism and shove it up your @#* between date number 567 and 568.

My quest for wholeness had its ups and downs. Around the time that I made that entry, I was sitting in a doctor's office, where my revelations seem to take place, reading a magazine. I was thinking how everyone seems to wonder at some point in his or her life or at many points in their life who they are. Usually as a teenager, again in your twenties, then in middle age with the middle age crisis, and perhaps around retirement. As we live, things happen; we change, grow, and have to rediscover who we are all over again sometimes. So how do we know who we are? Is there a simple answer to that question or is it so complex I'll have to pay thousands of dollars to a therapist to figure it out? I found the answer in an advertisement of all places. Those marketing geniuses and advertising executives have all of life's answers! Who knew? It was a runner's magazine, of course, as runners have all the answers as well (*that* I already knew). There was an ad with big red lettering that said: *It's what we love that defines us.*[3] The clouds parted, the heavens opened, and rays of sunshine shone down on me. A choir began to sing right there in the doctors office. Without thinking, I tore the page out of the magazine, and as luck (or fate!) would have it, the doctor walked in at that exact moment.

---
[3] Advertisement, *Runner's World* (2004).

"Umm, sorry, but I need this page, doctor. It has the meaning of life on it."

The doctor peered over his half-moon spectacles at me with a slightly amused look that may actually have been a smirk and gave me an unenthusiastic lets-get-on-with-it nod. I'm sure he thought I was crazy.

Upon further research, I discovered that the meaning of life I had found in the magazine had originated in the eighteenth century and had not been authored by the advertisement executives. German playwright, poet, and philospher Johann Wolfgang von Goethe originally said, "We are shaped and fashioned by what we love." It seemed that hundreds of years ago they had discovered that which I was searching for.

It's what we love that defines us. It's the qualities that we choose to be that define us. It's our choices that define us. It is our voice inside of us telling us what we like and don't like. It's our voice inside making choices for ourselves. It's not our surroundings or environment or upbringing or addictions or crutches, and it's not our family and friends. That is not who we are. It's not our soul mate or significant other. It's what you *love*. It's your Empowering choices. It's what you choose for yourself. That is who you are. It is not *who* you love but *what* you love. It's the things that you spend your time doing, activities that you spend your time pursuing and ideas that you spend your time thinking about. Life is just made up of time, after all. That's all you get. I know who I am now! I know who I am because I know what I love, and I love those things with such intense passion, determination, fervor, and obsession that there is absolutely no mistaking it. I love what I love. Nothing else matters. I choose to spend my time, my effort, my days, my afternoons, and my weekends pursuing the things that I love. I choose to embrace my interests, my hobbies, and my pastimes and to let those things become my identity. I choose life.

I choose to be a whole person and not a half person—always.

I raced home from the doctor's office that day and wrote feverishly in my journal. I made a list of things that I love and a list of things that I love to do. Just to name a few, I love: music, heavy metal, concerts, quotations, poetry, running marathons, traveling, sightseeing, American history, learning, quilting, sewing, World War II history, my Iwo Jima flag-raising statue, Disneyworld, REO Speedwagon, movies, teaching, sight-seeing, writing, reading, exercising, cheese pizza, and candy corn.

My path of self-discovery continues, and I don't know what the future holds. But I do know that I will continue to embrace the things that I love; I will make no excuses for them, and I will let them fill me up and fill up my days and nights. I will be defined by them. And if a significant other does come my way, great. If not, not only will I survive, I will thrive because I am a whole person. If he does come along though, he has to love me for who I am because I am not going to ever pretend to be something that I am not just to earn someone's love. I will be defined by and be proud of the characteristics I love about myself, and I accept my imperfections. I will make Empowering Choices for myself, and my pride and self-knowledge will be my armor against any storms that come my way. My journal of self-discovery continues, as we are never done growing and learning. I wrote the following poem in the journal:

    I am the only me
    That will ever be
    The only Sara
    Under the sun
    My spirit shines brightly
    There is fire inside
    There is hope
    There is promise
    There is strength
    There is pride
    I know what I know
    And I love what I love
    My passions consume me
    And fit like a glove
    Like a small spark
    Or a flame in the wind
    I gather my strength
    And refuse to give in
    I am a whole person

CHAPTER 6:
A LITTLE SAUSAGE

When I was a little girl I dreamed of having my own baby. I think every little girl has that dream; it's the reason toy makers make baby dolls—so little girls can play mommy. I had a doll called Whoopsie, and when you squeezed her tummy her pigtails would flop up. Then I had two Cabbage Patch dolls named Sam and Lisa. My best friend and I spent hours playing with our dolls; we would dress them up, give them fancy names like Lenore and Delilah, and rock them to sleep. As a teenager, I loved to watch shows or movies that depicted a birthing scene. I was mesmerized with the whole process: the brave strong woman, the supportive, loving husband, and the final scene with the slimy, wriggly little thing placed in the sweat-covered, exhausted mother's arms. Then the family gazing through the window at all the bassinets with the babies wrapped up like sausages—little sausages of love, hold the ketchup and mustard. I dreamed of the day I would be that brave, strong woman, exhausted and sweat-covered, with my supportive husband and my own little wrapped-up sausage. The sausage's big round eyes would gaze up at me from its enclosure, with complete trust and wonder. My friends and I used to always talk about what the baby's room would look like, how many babies we wanted, what order we wanted them in, and what sex we wanted first. We had the names all picked out, of course. One girlfriend would say, "I am getting married when I am twenty-five, then I am having my first one, a boy, at twenty-seven, and I will name him David, after my grandfather. Then I will have a girl three years later." Each of us in turn would declare the exact age at which each life event would happen. It's like we were at a restaurant placing our orders for the future.

We had our whole lives planned. But I guess no one told us that life just doesn't always work that way. Life is not a restaurant, and it doesn't take special orders.

There are some choices that are beyond our control. There's only so much you can choose for yourself in life, and the rest you have to leave to chance, fate, God, destiny, the four winds, luck, or whatever it is you believe in. As for myself, I go back and forth on the subject. When I'm having a good day, I have hope that there is a plan for me, a destiny, and my choices will lead me in the right direction to the right path. When I'm having a bad day, I believe that it's all chance, and fate is just wishful thinking. I decide to focus my good thoughts and positive energies on the things that I can control and forget about anything else. I will not let anything beyond my control consume my energy. Then when I am having one of those really bad, awful days that we all do sometimes, I get tired of being strong, brave, and optimistic, and I just let pessimism, negativity, and hopelessness wash over me like a warm blanket. I bathe in it, let it consume me, fill me up like hot chocolate on a cold night, and I immerse myself in the secure comfort of despair. I eventually snap out of it.

So as a child, I dreamed of a baby and pretended with my dolls; as a teenager, I was awed by the miracle of birth and placed my order at the restaurant of life. In my twenties, I simply stood by and watched as every one of my friends got married and had sausages of their own. It all started when I was about twenty-five-years-old. My sorority sisters from college would call me to say, "I have great news! You're not going to believe it! I am getting married! Will you be in my wedding?" It was exciting, and I happily helped plan bridal showers and wedding arrangements. I bought the appropriate dress in a matching color, got the alternations, and purchased the shoes in the right style and color. I got my hair and makeup done, walked up the aisle with my little bouquet, and helped the bride adjust her train. It was all very exciting the first time, and perhaps the second, and maybe even the third. It started to get old by the fourth or fifth time. It was downright annoying the sixth and seventh times. Anyone else who asks me to be a bridesmaid will have to shove it (kidding, girlfriends—I'm honored, really).

To date, I have seven bridesmaid dresses hanging in the back of my closet. Three of them are almost the exact same shade of lavender. I have one that I actually wore again a second time. On an optimistic day, I would say, "Oh, I am so lucky to have such wonderful, close friends! I am so blessed with loyalty and friendship." On a pessimistic day I would say, "When in the *#% is it going to be my turn?"

So once all of the girlfriends were married, it was not too long after that I started getting the phone calls about sausages. "I have great news! You're not going to believe it! I'm pregnant! Oh, Sara, will you help with the baby shower? You are so creative and good at that kind of stuff! Will you make me a baby quilt?" Again, I was genuinely happy for them—I could hear the thrill and delight in their voices. I would put on a smile and bury my envy deep down. My time would come. All things come to those who wait. I am still young. I have plenty of time. There are plenty of fish in the sea. I needed to be patient, and before I knew it, I would be holding a wrapped-up little sausage of my very own. I would be rocking it to sleep while humming a Metallica song (kidding—I know a few lullabies).

Well, this continued phone call after phone call, baby shower after baby shower. Soon I was getting phone calls that a second child was on the way. I made visits to the hospital, and visits to see the nursery and the adorable baby clothes and little baby things. I sewed flannel baby blankets, and purchased cute little outfits and accessories from baby registries. On and on and on. I continued to tell myself to be patient and be happy for them. But I woke up one day and realized something: I am so tired of people having babies that I have become bitter and resentful. Why them and not me? I deserve it too. It's my turn. I did not like who I had become. I used to love babies, and now I would roll my eyes and retreat at the mere mention of the word. This is not me. I do not want to be this person; I do not want to be bitter and resentful. I had to put a stop to it, and I had to change. But I couldn't help my feelings, so how do I change it? The fact is, they are all having babies, and it is something that I want. I needed to know that it would be in my future. I didn't have to have a sausage tomorrow or next week, but I wanted assurance that life would not pass me by without the opportunity to have one someday.

You are not going to believe where I was when the revelation of my Empowering Choice came to me. I know it sounds like I'm making this up, and it's crazy that all of my light bulb moments would occur at doctors offices, but that's where I was. I don't even go to doctors that much, actually. I was at the doctor's office and sitting on the table waiting for her to come in. It was the gynecologist, so there were diagrams of pregnancies hanging on the walls. I thought about the possibility of never finding Mr. Right and not having a baby or not finding him until it was too

late. Then I thought, what if I just decide that I am going to have a baby someday? What if I just decide that I am not going to go my entire life and not ever know the feeling of holding my baby in my arms? What if I just decide that? That's when I made an Empowering Choice:
I am going to have a baby.

The doctor walked in and I said, "I'm going to have a baby."

"Well, that's not what it says here in your chart, Ms. Wolf."

"Oh, I didn't mean today. I mean someday. You see, I'm waiting around for Mr. Right, but I only seem to be meeting plenty of Mr. Wrongs. I've decided that if Mr. Right does not come along by a certain age, I would like to have a little sausage, I mean a baby, on my own."

The doctor discussed when a good age would be to start trying on my own, and when it might be too late. Discussing the details with an actual doctor made the prospect *real*. I made a choice to do it because I can't imagine my entire life passing me by without experiencing the miracle of birth. I can't imagine living my whole life and not having a child and being a mommy. But saying it to myself and actually proclaiming it to the doctor were two different things. Was I giving up on love? Was I giving up on the possibility of ever getting married and living happily ever after by deciding to have a baby on my own someday? I guess that deep down in my heart of hearts I was hoping and even assuming that it would never actually come to that. I still hope that it won't. But having a baby on my own is not giving up on love. In fact, I will still have my whole life ahead of me. Who's to say I still won't find love after I've had the little sausage? Life won't end then and there. I would prefer to have a significant other with whom to share the experience of pregnancy and child rearing. Of course I would prefer the supportive, loving husband kissing my sweaty forehead when the nurse places the wrapped-up little sausage in my arms for the first time. I want the panicky husband to be gripping the wheel on the first ride home from the hospital, nervous because his entire world is in that car. I want someone lying beside me at night when we hear the crying for the 2:00 A.M. feeding. I want to see him rock our sausage to sleep, make funny faces to get it to laugh, and change the icky diapers. But I believe it was a rather famous rock band that informed me early on that we can't always get what we want, but if we try, sometimes we find that we get what we need (thanks Rolling Stones for that timeless wisdom).[1]

I want someone with whom to share the experience, but I cannot make a choice to wait for that person to have a baby because so much of it is out of my hands. I can hope, pray and put myself out there, but I cannot settle for less than I deserve in a relationship. I cannot conjure love out of thin air, and I cannot force it. I've read all the books, and I have spent a long time working on and becoming an open-minded, nonjudgmental person who doesn't overanalyze, cling to unrealistic expectations, or have impossible standards. I have spent a long time improving myself when it comes to meeting people and I feel confident about it now. But nonetheless, I cannot control the turning of the Earth on its orbit, sorry to say. All I can do is take action and hope for the best. In the meantime, I decided that I will eventually have the sausage, and if it needs

---

[1] The Rolling Stones, "You Can't Always Get What you Want," *Let it Bleed*, 1969, Decca Records.

to be on my own, that is how it has to be. Would I like support, emotionally, physically, financially, and in every other way? You bet. But I can and I will do it on my own if I must. That is what making an Empowering Choice is all about, after all. I am sure that it is the right path for me, the only acceptable path, and it isn't necessarily the easiest path to take, but it is mine, and I will pay the price, when the time comes. I will pay any price that I have to pay and bear the burden alone if need be because I know that this has to happen.

As I said, the revelation and final decision occurred at the doctor's office. As I wrestled with the logistics of my decision and contemplated what would be the right age to head down this road, I called one of my friends to proclaim the choice out loud. I just wanted to see how it sounded.

"If I have no romantic prospects by the time I am a certain age, I am going to have a baby on my own."

Now the friend on the other end of the line happens to be divorced with little ones of her own, so she knows a bit about the situation I was getting myself into.

"Will you still work while it is a baby? If not, how will you support yourself? Who will watch the baby when you go back to work? How will you afford daycare? Will it be an only child or will you want another one? Do you think your apartment is big enough or will you need to move?" my friend asked.

After the barrage of questions ended, I fell silent. I was stunned. I had not considered all of that. Actually, I hadn't made it past the idea of the miracle of birth and holding the baby as I sat in a rocking chair.

"Umm, I hadn't really thought it out, I guess. But I'll cross those bridges when I come to them. I'll figure all of those things out one at a time."

I know that I am more than capable of being a good parent, with the support of a partner or without it. The time will come, and I will have a baby of my own. I know I will because I had made a choice. I am armed with my decision, and I am empowered. I know that this is the path I will go down. I have too much love to give to a child, and too much experience, knowledge, and support to give to another human being. I was born to be a parent. It will happen. When I go out on a date, I do not have to feel anxious or pressured or desperate in any way. I can just go out and get to know someone, have a good time, and enjoy the moment. I do not have to wonder if this guy is good daddy material. It doesn't matter if he is or not because I don't need him to have a baby. Now that I know that the baby will happen, I no longer have to dread the phone calls I get when a girlfriend tells me she's pregnant. I no longer have to detest baby showers and shopping for baby gifts. I do not have to cry out in despair and ask why they deserve it and have it, and I don't. I deserve it too, and I will make it happen. That's right—I will not sit back on my couch, and hope and pray. That is not how you make dreams come true. You make them come true by getting up off of your duff, making a choice, and going after it. That is the kind of person I have made up my mind to be. I am not a person to whom life happens; I am a person who makes life happen. I do not look up at night and wish upon stars and wait for the fairy godmother to grant my wishes. I start building myself a strong ladder, so I can reach for those stars.

"Would you like bacon or sausage with your eggs, ma'am?"

"I'll take a sausage."

CHAPTER 7: NO VICTIMS

I am an elementary school teacher. Each year in January, around Martin Luther King Day, I teach a unit to my kids about the life and legacy of Dr. King. As soon as they find out he was killed, they want to know all the gory details. But I tell my students that how he died is not as important as how he lived, what he stood for, what he fought for, and what he died for. On April 3, 1968, Dr. Martin Luther King, Jr. gave a speech titled "I've been to the Mountaintop" in which he said "And I've seen the Promised Land. I may not get there with you. But I want you to know tonight, that we, as a people, will get to the Promised Land."[1]

Dr. King was assassinated the very next day. He didn't see his dream realized, but he made it possible for others. He forged the path for so many people, and as a teacher, an American, and a human being, I am inspired by his legacy. I instill his teachings in my students each year, and I teach them that the right thing is not always the easy thing. I tell my students that if they take away nothing else from my lessons, they must take away the lessons of that man. He was not a victim. He taught us all to follow our dreams and stay our course in the face of opposition. Stand up for what is right even if you are the only one standing. Never give up on your dreams. Believe in yourself and believe in the goodness of others. Believe that although there is both good and evil in this world, and although men are capable of unspeakable acts, everyone is capable of incredible selflessness and compassion. Dr. King lived and died for his beliefs, and amazingly, he proclaimed that he did not hate his enemies. People despised him, said vile

---

[1] Martin Luther King, Jr. "I've Been to the Mountaintop." Speech in support of Sanitation Workers, Church of God in Christ Headquarters, Memphis, Tennessee, 3 April 1968.

and horrible things to him, were racially prejudiced and bigoted, threatened him and his family, and targeted him with violence. He did not hate these people. Inspired by Mahatma Gandhi's nonviolent demonstrations, Dr. King taught that you can't overcome the circumstances of oppression with hate and violence; only love and understanding could overcome oppression. He was not a victim because he made a choice not to be.

My first conscious memory of feeling like a victim was when I was in the first grade. There was a girl named Micki who I liked and admired. I wanted to be her friend, but she was always mean to me. She made me feel like I was not good enough to be her friend. My friend Laura was nice to me unless Micki was around. On one beautiful spring day we were on the elementary school playground, and I was playing on the swing. I was happy and content in my own little world. Then I spotted Micki, Laura, and a third girl. They had formed a circle, holding hands with their arms crossed over one another in a tight bond. Linked together, the girls were walking around the playground in this tight knit circle, and Micki kept looking my way just to taunt me. So I took the bait, went over to them, and asked if I could join in. "No way," Micki said, "You are not part of our circle. You can only have three in this circle." I was so crushed. I ran up to the teacher in tears and said that it wasn't fair that they would not let me play. The teacher said to find something else to play. I walked in circles around the three girls, stalking them like a hawk and wishing that I could join their game. They kept looking at me and laughing. I just kept thinking, "It's not fair. It's not fair. Why don't they like me?"

We cannot control others. We cannot control what other people say, do, or feel. We can only exert so much influence over others, and then it is up to them to act. We can only control ourselves. As a child in elementary school, I discovered early on that there were nice people who wanted to be my friend, and there were mean people who did not. And then there were people who pretended to be my friend but were really just out for themselves and did not have my best interest at heart. To me, these were the worst kind of people. At least with the mean people, you knew exactly where you stood. But with the pretenders, you could not always tell whether to trust them or not. Sometimes pretenders were wonderful actors, and you thought they were true and loyal, but they would eventually show their true colors. When these people fooled me into believing that I could trust them, I felt betrayed and belittled; I realized that they were just like the mean people on the inside. I felt three inches tall. And the worst part is, I was desperate for their acceptance and approval.

It was not enough to have the acceptance and friendship of the nice people who were my true friends. I couldn't stand the idea that there was someone out there who did not like me and did not approve of me. Just knowing such a person existed and that there was nothing I could do about it bothered me. I would be preoccupied with it so much that I lost sight of the true friendship that was staring me right in the face. Time and time again I would let these people bother me, while they would just go on with their lives and not even care. I was a victim, and I was absolutely letting myself be a victim. By craving and desiring the acceptance of people who didn't like me, I was allowing myself to become a victim. But I blamed them! It was their fault, you see, because they had no reason in the world not to like me. I was nice to them, I said kind things, I payed them compliments, and I was helpful and sweet. I even tried acting aloof and impartial. None of it mattered. They just didn't like me, and there was no reason for it. There was nothing I did or didn't do to cause it, and nothing was going to change it. But I simply couldn't see and didn't realize that I was allowing myself to become a victim. I thought that they were putting me in this position and it was their fault, but it was really my fault. I was putting myself in the situation and letting myself be their victim by letting it bother me so much.

I can remember the faces and names of these pretenders and mean people in elementary school, middle school, high school, and college. They exerted so much influence on my state of mind from childhood into adulthood. When I was in the sixth grade I got a huge cloth patch of the rock band Poison and sewed it to the back of my jean jacket. I was so excited and proud, and I couldn't wait to wear it to school. So there I was on the playground in my new Poison jacket with my head held high, feeling like the coolest act in town. And then I saw these two girls who were always mean and nasty to me. One of them was actually a huge Poison fan, so she assumed that I got the jacket just to make her jealous. So they came up to me, and started teasing and taunting me about it. I think that was the first and last time I wore my Poison jacket. By the way, I have seen Poison a dozen times or more since then, mostly in the last five years or so. So who's the real fan, huh?

And then one particular incident changed everything. I realized what was happening. It all started with a particular person with whom I worked. Let's call her Tracy. I had just gotten a new job, and I was ready to work hard. I was bright eyed and bushy tailed, and prepared to take on the world. I assumed that everyone at my new job would want to instantly be my best friend, show me the ropes, and welcome me with open arms. And everyone did, except Tracy. Oh, she was not overtly nasty or mean to me. She didn't sneer at me or make rude remarks. She just spoke to me when she needed to, worked with me and alongside me as required by the job, and did not make any small talk whatsoever. There was always coldness, unfriendliness, and an obvious aloofness in the air. It was clear that she worked with me only because she had to but was not interested whatsoever in being friendly or chummy. It wasn't enough for me that everyone else I worked with was as kind as could be, warm, and friendly. It only bothered me that there was this one person who had just decided that she did not care for me. There was no reason for it, so I tried to win her over. I tried killing her with kindness. I would be especially friendly, helpful, and supportive in the work environment. I would attempt to make small talk, show interest and respect, and just be a warm buttery little muffin to her. Nope. The icy exterior did not show any sign of warming. Then I tried acting indifferent, pouring myself into my work with dedication and passion, hoping that when she saw I was not trying so hard anymore, she would break. Nope. Not even a single crack. I remember another coworker coming in one day, and I just broke down on her shoulder, filled with such frustration, anger, and resentment. I did not want to be Tracy's best friend and share warm cozy nights with her; I just wanted her to be friendly to me. I wanted her to like me. I respected her as a colleague and admired her work, and I wanted her to feel that respect toward me as well. Then I tried calling her up and being open about the whole situation and explaining how I felt. It was an appeal for a truce and a fresh start. So Tracy said to me, "I will always be cordial to you, Sara." Well that was my answer. I loved my job. I felt confident in my abilities, I was growing and learning, I felt needed and appreciated, and I looked forward to getting up and going to work. But this one person was ruining the entire experience for me. Her coldness and dislike of me was all I could think about or focus on. I was completely miserable and angry, and it was eating me up inside. How could this one person have so much control over me? How did she get the ability to have such an affect on my life and happiness? What right does she have to treat me as she does? *Who* gave her such enormous control over me?

I did.

I let her have the control. I was letting this ruin a situation and opportunity that was wonderful and perfect in every other respect. I pictured her sitting at home after work, going about her life, doing her job each day; I realized that she was not affected by this at all. The situation was not consuming her thoughts, it was not conversation at her dinner table, and it was not keeping her up at night. She could care less about it. I was letting the situation overtake my own life. I was allowing myself to be victimized. I realized that I had been letting myself be a victim my whole life, since that first incident on the first grade playground. It was then that I made an Empowering Choice:

I will not let myself be a victim. I will not let the actions and attitudes of others take over my life and destroy my happiness. I will rise above it.

I realized what had been happening for so long—since childhood. I realized that I could control these feelings, and I could do something about it by making an Empowering Choice. Part of changing my attitude involved accepting that I could choose not to be a victim, but I also needed to realize that I did not need the acceptance and approval of the pretenders or the mean people. I had to be okay going along in the world and living my life day to day knowing that there was a person out there who did not like me. Either she had a good reason not to like me, a bad reason not to like me, or no reason at all. It didn't matter. She just didn't like me, and I had to accept that and live with it. It didn't matter if she liked me or not because *I like me*. I accept me. I approve of me. I love me. I respect me. I have friends and family who do love me unconditionally, and I do not need the support of those who do not. I do not need their approval to feel like a whole person. If they do not like me, it is their loss. It's a big world, and there are plenty of people in it. This life is much too short to spend precious time and energy on things that will poison me or bring me down. Those people can go on with their lives, and I can go on with mine.

I remember once I decided to throw myself a birthday party. I was in my twenties and had just graduated college several years before. I had a new apartment and wanted everyone to see it. I invited lots of people, bought a ton of food, got drinks, wine, and a cake, put up decorations, and made lots of preparations. I made so many plans and looked forward to it for so long. The day of the party came, and people began to trickle in. I kept saying that it was still early, and more people would come. They were just being fashionably late. But they didn't come. Only a handful of people came. There were so many people who bailed out and did not come to my party. Why didn't they come?

They don't like me? They don't think my party's worth attending? They assume that it will be boring or no fun because it is my party? They had something better to do that night? All of the questions and doubts I had involving the absence of my guests showed self-doubt. They reflected something wrong with me. They showed a lack of self-worth. I took their actions personally when it may have been that they just couldn't make it for whatever reason. I will never forget what a friend of mine who was at the party said: "Why don't you enjoy the people who *are* here instead of focusing on those who are not?"

Sometimes one tiny little comment that a person makes can make all the difference. It was just one little passing remark, but I remember it often and refer to its wisdom in many situations. Focus on the people who did come to the party. Focus on the friends who wanted to be there for my birthday. Enjoy the company of those around me. Enjoy my own company. Do not let the actions or inactions of others spoil the moment. Do not let my good time and happy mood be ruined by another person's absence, bad attitude, or downright rudeness. Focus on what is right in front of your face instead of the images or fantasies you pictured in your head. Focus on the donut and not on the hole. Enjoy the family and friends that love you, enjoy the blessings in your life, and enjoy the qualities in yourself that you are proud of. Forget the rest—just *let it go*.

CHAPTER 8: THE VOICE INSIDE

I was looking through my old high school yearbooks recently. As is the custom, friends and classmates wrote messages in the binding of the book. It's funny, you know, at the time you think they are your best friends and you'll stay in touch forever, but life has other plans I guess. I rarely talk to any of those people anymore, and I didn't even recognize some of the names. I noticed a recurring theme in the inscriptions: don't ever change. Why do we write this in yearbooks? We know that life is about to change drastically, and we are about to go and take on the big, bad world. We think we know who we are and what we want, and we step out in a direction with confidence and purpose. We tell each other not to change and not to let outside influences and life experiences alter who we are, our beliefs, our standards, our character traits, and our nature. But even as we are saying it, we know it's going to happen. We change. We have to.

We live in a world of labels. People label their clothes, their music, their social status, and their rung on the career ladder. I remember as a teenager first discovering the different labels and genres of music: classic, oldies, country, alternative, heavy metal, rock n' roll, blues, jazz, rap, pop, and the list goes on and on. But one summer I went to the Rock N' Roll Hall of Fame and Museum in Cleveland, Ohio, and it was there that I discovered something. At the Rock N' Roll Museum, it was all just music. All of the labels faded away and they didn't matter anymore. Everybody from Elvis to Styx and all the bands between were all one and the same there. It was all just Rock N' Roll. In high school, there were preps, jocks, nerds, hand bangers, and other labels. You have a label, and you are defined by it.

It is who you are. Then you go to college, and the labels are still there, but less important. As an adult, I realized that labels don't matter. It is not who you are. Who you are is the person inside, the voice in your head, the gut instinct that tells you what you like, what you want, what you love, what you hate, what you believe, what you think, and what you want to be when you grow up. You are the voice inside you. Isn't that funny? The voice inside you is the only thing that you have constant company of, your whole entire life, and every second of every day from the moment you are born until the moment you die. Every single other thing comes and goes: people, parents, lovers, rewards, accomplishments, degrees, jobs, money, cars, and clothes. The only thing you really own and possess is you – the voice inside you. It is what defines you. It is who you are. And it is enough! There are so many people who feel that who they are inside is not good enough and they need accomplishments and possessions to feel self-worth. They earn degrees, earn more money, lose weight, get honors and awards, and get big houses or big cars. Maybe you are one of those people.

The bottom line is you have to believe that who you are inside is good enough and that you are worthy of respect and love just as you are. As you grow and experience life, it changes. Change is inevitable. You take on different personas, you change your beliefs, you adopt new mottoes to live by, you take on new interests and let other interests go, and sometimes you even change your morals and belief systems. In our high school yearbooks we write, "don't change" because it's a time in life when you are scared. The future is so uncertain and there are so many choices and so many paths. It is a terrifying prospect and so we tell our friends to stay the same person that they are now and not to let all of the outside influences change who they are inside. We want to stay safe and warm inside our little cocoons. We are so scared of all of the change that is about to take place that we are in denial of it and we tell each other, "No! No changing! No changing! No changing!"

But we do change. And even through all the life experiences and all the changes, we still have the voice inside telling us which is the right path for us and which choices we should make. Sometimes people stop paying attention to their voice and become clouded by outside voices, or you may let one particular thing dominate your life and become central to your identity. I learned several times in my life not to let my character and who I was be defined by one particular person, object, or interest. If that person or interest is removed, as may be inevitable, you may have an identity crisis because you don't know who you are anymore. But sometimes it's so easy to let one thing take over your whole identity and your whole being because it feels so natural to let it become who you are. It has to be an Empowering Choice to value and respect who you are on the inside. You have to choose to recognize that who you are on the inside is enough.

When I was in high school I was a head banger (someone who like heavy-metal music). That was my label. I had liked heavy-metal music from the time I was in sixth grade. By the eighth grade, I had every inch of wall space papered with posters of my favorite heavy metal heroes, with their long hair and torn black T-shirts. I had stacks of metal magazines, CDs, and paraphernalia. I hung out with a crowd who also loved that music and dressed the part. In the ninth grade, my parents decided that this was a path that they did not want their sweet little girl taking. They put a stop to it in a major way. No more heavy-metal friends, heavy-metal T-shirts, heavy-metal posters, or heavy-metal identity. It broke my heavy-metal heart. My friends and belongings had become the sum of my identity, and that influence was obscuring my voice. I didn't know who I was without the heavy-metal lifestyle. It took me a very long time to realize that there was only one thing that was important in all of this mess—music.

I became aware that the voice inside me was telling me that music was in my soul and part of my spirit. The friends, the T-shirts, the posters, and all of that stuff did not matter one little bit. The music was inside me then, it always was, and it still is today. It cannot be removed. I will always have music inside of me. Sometimes I am thinking of a song inside my head, and I can hear it playing in my brain so clearly that it's just as if I have earphones on! It's really crazy, actually. So now I dress conservatively (sometimes), and I look totally normal, but I like to go to Metallica and Megadeth concerts. In fact, I am absolutely in heaven when I am at a Metallica or Megadeth concert! (Oh, that reminds me, I have to get tickets for a show coming up in January!) I don't have to look the part. I don't have to dye my hair blue, get body piercings and tattoos, or wear black T-shirts with skulls on them. There was a student at the school where I worked with whom I made a special connection because of a shared love of music. We were always stopping in the hall to talk about a concert or a song. When the student was going through a hard time, I told him that music was inside of him and would always be there when he needed it. It's enough to have it inside of me. The music is enough.

When I was a teenager my mom wrote a poem for me called "The Voice"

There's a silent voice that you will hear
Whispering quietly in your ear
It will come to you...someday...some night
When you least expect it
When the time is right
It will be your guide and lead you to
The path that's right and best for you
There's a silent voice
I know it's true
Many times in my life I've heard it too
It's not my voice you'll hear, my dear
You'll hear your own voice...loud and clear

When I read that poem, I made an Empowering Choice: *I will always listen to my voice, and I will always be true to myself.*

If you listen to yourself deep down inside above all others and trust what you have to say, then you are being true to yourself. Sometimes when I'm not sure about a decision that needs to be made, I'll ask everyone I know for their opinion. But then I'll realize that I'm just looking for outside support and confirmation when the real answer is inside of me. I come first. My voice inside knows what I like, and it knows what I don't like; it's my job to shut out everyone around me and listen to that voice. I am number one. I know what's best for me, and I have to trust that. I have to trust myself. That actually reminds me of a Metallica lyric: "Forever trusting who we are, and nothing else matters."[1] There is nothing else. There is only you, and you come first. That settles it then. Runners and heavy-metal bands have all the answers to life's questions!

You know, it's funny, but I remember looking in the mirror when I was little and thinking, "That's me in there. Why am I me? Why am I in there, and how did I get in there?" I found it so weird to think that I was born as me, Sara, inside this body, and I am nobody else. Mom is mom. Dad is dad. My brother is my brother. The president is the president, and I am me. I got out of bed every morning, and guess who's there? Me. I look in the mirror every day, and who's there? Me. I eat and play and read and talk and watch TV and when I go to bed every night who is in there still? Who is always there every second of every day? Me. But why was I born me and not someone else? How did I get in there? Okay, now I'm getting a little too deep. I am not a philosopher, and I don't have the answers to these questions. All I know is that I am in there, and if I don't make good choices on my own behalf, respect myself, and listen to myself, then I shouldn't expect anyone else to either.

I am in charge of me. I am the one who decides. And on that note, I do not owe anyone explanations or excuses for the decisions that I make. My friend Brook is always calling me when she needs an excuse to get out of some plans that she has made. Whether it's a date or hanging out with a friend who is visiting town for a few days, Brook has a small problem with telling a little white lie, such as, "I am not feeling well." I told her that she does not have to explain herself or give any reason or excuse for the decisions she makes. You simply say, "It's just not going to work out." Well, she pressed me further and asked, what if

---
[1] Metallica, "Nothing Else Matters," *The Black Album*, 1992, Elektra.

they ask why? Then you repeat, "I'm so sorry I can't make it, but it's just not going to work out this time." The end. You made a choice. You made a decision. Whether we are talking about getting out of a dinner date or a life-altering decision, you are in charge of you, and you do not owe anyone explanations. You have to trust in yourself that you know what is best for you, and that's the end of the story. Life is too short to burden yourself with explanations. Now Brook refers to this as the *Sara method* of getting out of something: "It's just not going to work out." Try it sometime. It works in lots of situations. When Brook needed to tell someone that she was moving out of the state, she felt compelled to give a reason. I told her to say, "I have given this a lot of thought, and I know it's the right decision for me." If you listened to your voice inside and you made a decision, you do not owe explanations. So when I decided that this is the kind of music I like, and running is something that I have to do, I was listening to my voice inside and that was enough. I did not have to give an explanation for it. Why do I have to blast my music in the car on the way to work? Why do I have to spend hundreds of dollars in physical therapy, so I can run again? I just do. No explanation necessary. And what if I can't listen to the music anymore for some reason? What if I am permanently injured and can't run anymore? Then I'm still me. I'm still Sara, and I still have my voice. I will always have the joys and memories of the music and the running inside of me, whether or not I can experience them again.

 When I had my running injury, I learned again not to let my character be defined by one particular interest. I had a bit of an identity crisis. Running marathons and just running in general had become so much a part of who I was. If I was in a good mood, I would go for a run. If I was in a bad mood, I would go for a run. If I was grumpy, angry, depressed, or frustrated, a run was exactly what I needed. If I saw someone I hadn't seen in a while they would say, "Hey how ya doin' Sara? Run any marathons lately?" After the injury, I was faced with the possibility of never being a runner again. What would I do if I couldn't run anymore? Who would I be if I was not a runner? One night, I sent my best running buddy Cherise the following text: "I am not a runner anymore. If I am not a runner, who am I?" Cherise responded: "You will run again. But even if you don't, you will always be a runner. It's inside of you. You are still you." And I realized that running was not who I was. It was just something that I did, and if it was taken away, I would still be me. My accomplishments involving running would always be there. I realized that you can't let one single thing totally take you over. Running is a part of my voice inside just as music and many other things are. They all fit together like a puzzle to make up me. Change happens. Life happens. Things that you absolutely don't want to happen…happen. But you will always have you. That will never change. I am my own best friend. I am my voice.

CHAPTER 9:
IT'S JUST A ROCK

I have always been somewhat of a pack rat, I suppose. I collect things, store them away, and hang onto them. The other day my mom was cleaning out her closets and garage. She called and told me that there were boxes full of stuff from my childhood. "You know, Sara," she said, "You should really go through this stuff and throw it away. There's no sense in hanging onto these things. It's just clutter."

Clutter? My precious childhood treasures are clutter? My Figment from Disney World, Yorgus and Roger, my Pound Puppies, and my fourth-grade report on Elvis Presley are not clutter. My old Bon Jovi VHS tapes, sticker books, high school assignment books, and notes I passed or received in junior high classes, old ballet slippers, and Gone With the Wind memorabilia are not clutter. They mean something. They are part of my childhood. They are my memories. They have value. This really got me thinking about what would become of this stuff. Will the boxes be transferred to my garage, where they'll sit and collect dust? Maybe I'll peek in a box or two once a decade, and after I pass away, it will pass into the hands of my children and grandchildren someday and they will go through the boxes and wonder at the junk I kept. Maybe they'll be intrigued by the stuff Grandma Sara saved from her childhood. They'll say, "Wow, what kind of tape is this? VHS? That's a real antique! Elvis Presley? Who was that?" Someday it will all sit in the garage of my children, grandchildren, or great grandchildren, if they are packrats like me. If they aren't packrats, everything will be thrown away into a dumpster somewhere.

It's funny how we cling to things and tell ourselves that things have meaning. We hold them, we save them, and we cherish them. We think that maybe a little part of ourselves is transferred into these things. I have a wedding ring and band that belonged to my grandmother that I wear sometimes. I am grateful to have something that was very important to her and that she wore everyday when she was alive. I almost did not get these rings. You see, my grandma lived in a senior living facility, and in the last few weeks of her life, the rings no longer fit and were lost. A few days after her passing, the cleaning crew found the rings as they were sweeping the floor. It is pretty amazing that they happened to spot the rings and knew to whom they belonged. I guess I was supposed to have them! If the rings could talk, I'm sure they would have an amazing story to tell. But they can't talk. I don't know where she got them or the circumstances under which they were given. But I know one thing—I will give them to my own daughter and tell her that they belonged to her great-grandmother Adina, an extraordinary lady indeed.

I have gotten better about my packrat ways, and I have discovered that I can let go of things. Some objects are for hanging onto for the long haul, and some objects aren't. People sometimes ask themselves what they would save if there was a fire in their home. Think about it. If there was a fire and you could only save one thing, assuming your family and pets were already safe, what would you grab? Many people have pondered this question before but a few unlucky people have faced it. People say that they would save photographs, important mementos, or family heirlooms that have been passed on from generation to generation. I've always contended that I would grab my running medals and the quilts that I made. That's a lot of things to haul off at a moment's notice. I actually had a fire in my condo, and the only thing I had the presence of mind to grab was the dog!

Do objects really have the meaning that we think they do, or do they only have meaning because we attach meaning to them ourselves? We think they have meaning, we tell ourselves that they do, and then eventually it is so engrained that we actually believe it and we are certain of it. We attach meaning to religious objects like a Bible, a cross, a star, or candlesticks. We attach meaning to trophies, medals, awards, and degrees that are hanging on our walls. We attach meaning to old toys, clothes, books, and jewelry that belong to loved ones. But I think that if you look deep inside yourself, you will find that the meaning is actually inside of you instead. If you look deep inside, in your heart and your soul, you'll find that it is enough! If I lost my marathon medals, would I be totally devastated? You bet. Runners are always joking to each that it's all about the medal. In *Marathoning for Mortals* John Bingham wrote, "Once they place that medal around your neck, no one can ever make you give it back."[1] But if I lost my medals would it take away the accomplishment of training for and completing the marathons? Would it negate the entire effort and erase its existence? Would it mean that it never happened? The answer is no. Runners say that it's all about the medal, but we know deep down that it's really not. We know that the real reward is the feeling inside of you that comes with knowing that you've actually done this thing that you set out to do. It's the feeling that can't be described to anyone who hasn't finished a marathon. Marathon finishers carry around that feeling for the rest

---

[1] Bradley, James, and Ron Powers. *Flags of Our Fathers*. Reissue ed. United States and Canada: Bantam, 2006.

of their lives, and they know that they can achieve the impossible and tackle anything that comes their way. They know because they have already done it— medals or no medals.

Our sacred objects are wonderful and important and nice to have. But if you search inside yourself, you'll find that it's enough to have the meaning in your heart, and you don't need those objects to remind you of it. It's all about having some perspective. It is enough to remember the person, event, or belief that the object represents and to have that memory inside. Your whole life, from the time you're born and all of your natural days, right up until you die, that's what you have! When you die, you can't take the book or necklace or photographs with you! You came into this world alone and you're going to leave it alone—that's the cold, hard truth folks! What you have is YOU and that's all. That's it. All of these things that fill your house and to which you cling for dear life, and spend money on and organize, and get to impress your friends and neighbors— these are not you, and they are not the important thing. You have to be enough. Just you. You have to find the meaning inside of yourself and tell yourself that it is good enough and that's all. Amen. The end. Good night.

But wait, I'm not quite done yet.

A teacher who is a colleague of mine gives a rock to the students for the holidays each year. She has a big bowl with different kinds of rocks, and she tells the children that each rock has special meaning. She tells them about the Native Americans and their beliefs and customs concerning rocks. Some of them ward off illness or are associated with wisdom, and others are calming and soothing or protect you from evil spirits. I think this is a lovely idea, and I really love the way it is presented to the students. She told the students to shut their eyes tightly, clear their minds, and reach into the bowl. She told them to let their heart choose and their heart would guide them toward the right rock for them. Each child took a turn, squeezed his or her eyes real tightly, and with a look of pure concentration and absorption, reached into the bowl and plucked out one tiny rock. The children held their rocks in their hand as though it were a treasure they found at the end of the rainbow, gazed up at the teacher and asked, "What does it mean? What does it mean?"

Soon it was my turn. The children stared up at me, excited that their teacher was going to try. I figured, what could it hurt? So I squeezed my eyes shut, cleared my mind of all thoughts, and reached into the bowl. My fingers settled on a few rocks, but they didn't seem right. I moved my hand around a few more times and finally plucked one rock from the pile. I held a beautiful light pink rock in my hand, and the other teacher looked at it and said, "It's a rose quartz, Ms. Wolf. It's for love." She winked at me.

It worked! My heart must have really chosen that rock. Wow, what could be more perfect? I happen to be currently in the market for that very thing! Maybe someone up there is shining down on me after all! It was either divine intervention, luck, or a big fat coincidence. The teacher went on to tell the children that they should keep the rock in their pocket, and it would bring the quality it stands for. They should put it under their pillows at night and they would have good dreams.

So that very night I gave it a try. When I got into bed I had the rock on my bedside table and I tucked it under the pillow. My dog, who was dozing next to me, looked at me sheepishly from the corner of her eye and cocked an ear as if to say, "What in the *&% do you think you're doing?" So I said, "Hey, it can't hurt, right? I'm not exactly the princess and the pea."

I had a nightmare that night. I had a dream that my friend Brook and I were in Las Vegas in a hotel elevator. Brook is one of my closest, dearest friends, but we are very different in many ways—she is devoutly religious and orthodox and I'm not. Getting back to the nightmare, Brook and I were on the elevator with many other people when suddenly the elevator got stuck and we couldn't get off. We found a way to crawl out, but a bad man was there and wouldn't let us off the elevator, which was going to crash out from under us at any second. I managed to scramble out briefly, but the bad man chased me around and back into the elevator. I woke up in a sweat!

The next morning I thought about the dream and the rock. I usually have to call my good friend in Austin for dream interpretations, but this one I had all by myself. The elevator was love! My friend Brook happens to be just as single as I am. In fact, we commiserate on the phone all the time about our single status and the hopelessness of it all. The elevator was love or the lack thereof, and it was about to crash, and Brook and I couldn't get off. When I did get off, I was chased back on. In a sense, we were both just as screwed as the other one was, even though she was a believer and I wasn't. I called her the next day and told her about the dream. She didn't like it much. I don't think she'll be getting on an elevator with me anytime soon.

So I took my rock back to school and showed it to a coworker. I told her that it was for love and that I had put it under my pillow for good dreams about love. I told her about the elevator and what it meant. I said, "My rock is defective! It didn't work!" and do you know what she said? "Sara, it's a *rock*. That's all. It's just a rock."

Did I really believe that I would have good dreams and that the rock caused me to have a nightmare about an imminent disaster involving an elevator? Did I really believe that the rock stood for love and that the rock "chose" me? I guess not. But it was a lovely idea, and I figured it couldn't hurt. I might have told myself deep inside that I would dream about love and so my subconscious concocted this dream that showed my true feelings on the subject at the moment: that whether I believe it will happen or not, I seem to be screwed either way. Or it could be that because I recently went on a trip with Brook I was dreaming about going with her to Las Vegas! (There's no way she'll go there with me now or ever after that dream, by the way!)

It was just a rock. I attached meaning to it and told myself that it would give me good dreams about love. Maybe if I kept it in my pocket on a date, I would actually find love. But that is ridiculous because it's only a rock. I'm not saying that all possessions are meaningless and everyone should throw out there grandmother's old china. It is nice to have things that have been passed down from one generation to the next because they connect us with the past. We tell the stories associated with those things and keep the memory of that person alive. More than that, it's comforting to know that you are in possession of an actual object that belonged to your loved one. When I wear my grandmother's ring I think about her wearing the same ring and that it meant something to her. Treasures and mementos of loves ones are nice to have. But material possessions are not the most important things in life. Objects have meaning because we believe that they do but a little perspective is important. You don't need a tangible object to keep the memory of someone alive. You don't need expensive cars, medals, or a huge house full of expensive stuff to prove that you are a winner. You don't need medals and trophies and awards. You don't need a closet full of expensive clothes, shoes, or diamonds to make you important. You don't need to feel like you are not enough in and of yourself so you need to make yourself better by having stuff, stuff, and more stuff. You are enough. You are important, and you are enough. You don't need to hold onto things from years and years past to hold onto your childhood. Your childhood is inside of you. So my Empowering Choice is:

I will remember to put things into perspective. Stuff is just stuff and not the most important thing. I will remember that I am good enough. Just me.

You know, on my next break from work, I think I may go over to mom's house and throw away some of that old stuff in my storage boxes. I don't really need to save my old Bon Jovi videos from sixth grade or my eighth grade notes and letters. Then again, maybe I'll hang onto some of them. Just in case!

CHAPTER 10:
ON THE WAY TO BALLET

When I was about three-years-old, my mother put me in ballet and jazz classes. Once a week my mom would drive me out to Indian Hill, which was forty-five minutes from our house, and I would dance around in my little tights and leotard and act like a prima ballerina. I took ballet classes at the Dance Studio for the next ten years. Once a week became twice a week, and twice a week became three times a week. I graduated from ballet shoes to toe shoes. Once a year we had a big recital, and I wore fancy costumes, got my hair and makeup done, and danced around on a big stage. Going to ballet made me feel special and unique. I felt like this was something that made me stand out from the crowd, something that I could be proud of. At a young age, it taught me that exercise, activity, and movement were important for health and fitness—a lesson that has stuck. But I wasn't very good at ballet. I could learn all the steps and execute them, but I was not a natural born dancer. I did not have a dancer's body or dancer's feet. I knew that. The instructor knew that. I'm pretty sure my parents knew that too, although they never let on about it. When I was thirteen I realized how much time, effort, and money was being poured into this interest that I knew was not going to last. This was not an interest that I would continue throughout my life either as a career or a hobby. I had enjoyed it, but it had run its course.

Thinking about my experience with ballet makes me wonder why people become involved in certain interests and activities. Both children and adults have a million different activities to choose from: basketball, baseball, soccer, karate, tae kwon do, dancing, piano, violin, or some other musical instrument, chess, art, choir, acting, collecting things such as stamps, cooking, photography, fishing, knitting, jewelry making, and on and on and on. The list is endless! Some children have a different after-school activity every day of the week! Why do we taxi children around from activity to activity? Do we try out all of these things as children and young adults to experience different activities in the hope we'll discover our best fit? Or do we want to be cultured and well-rounded individuals with varied interests? Of course, there are those parents who are living vicariously through their children and push them into activities they had yearned to be part of as children. Maybe mom or dad always wanted to play the piano but never had the means, motive, or opportunity so they are going to make sure that little Johnny does, whether he likes it or not!

But with all of these activities, whether forced or chosen, some are continued throughout life and some are dropped at the first opportunity. When I was little I joined a bowling league with my brother, his friend, and my best friend Carla. It was the first day of bowling. Carla did great and got a good score. My brother and his friend did fairly well and enjoyed themselves. Guess what my score was? Zero! That's right! Zilch. I did not knock over a single pin! I got *all* gutter balls. Go ahead and laugh at me. I'm not offended, really. My bowling career was over before it started. Then there was the flute. In music class we could choose an instrument to learn, and I decided it would be cool to play the flute. So my parents took me to the music store and spent all kinds of money on my shiny new silver flute and a beautiful black, silk-lined case. How long did my flute career last? About a week or so. The flute found a lovely home in the back of the closet next to the bowling ball. So my mom thought karate lessons would be good for my brother and I. We bought the traditional gear and showed up on our first day looking tough as nails and ready to kick some wood. I lasted one day. Not exactly my style. Not that you know what your style is when you're ten-years-old, and that's the point. Parents drag their children to various activities, so the children can find their niche.

But how do you find the right activity for you? And what if you never find it? Why do we like the things we like? Some people clearly have natural-born talents and abilities, but what if they never discover them? What if Michael Jordan never tried playing basketball? What if Elton John never tried playing the piano? What if Andrea Bocelli never tried singing? What if Tom Hanks never tried acting? What if Mikhail Baryshnikov never tried ballet? What if there is something out there that I have natural talent for, but I haven't discovered it because it just never occurred to me to try it? Does "fate" guide us toward it or is it just luck? Here is the question that it all boils down to: Do we choose hobbies or do hobbies choose us?

One thing is certain. I was not born to play the flute, practice karate, or be a bowling champion. I wasn't born to dance on my toes on a stage. And although I am a four-time marathon finisher, I certainly was not born to be a runner either. Running is never easy for me, but I enjoy it anyway; I work hard at it, so I am able to run long distances. But even if I ran, stretched, trained, and practiced all day every day and had the best trainers in the world, I could never ever run the way Steve Prefontaine could run.

Maybe some people are born to do certain things and some are not. But just because you are not born to do it doesn't mean you can't choose to do it anyway! Ah, ha.

You can *empower* yourself and choose to do anything that you want to do. You just have to want it bad enough. So how do you know when you've found the right hobby? How do you know when it's one that's going to stick with you? The answer is you have to go with your gut instinct and follow your heart. And you can't give up when it gets hard. Sometimes the fact that it's hard is what makes it so wonderful and rewarding. In the movie *A League of Their Own*, Gina Davis plays a professional baseball player who is giving up baseball, a game that she has natural talent for. Gina Davis's character tells her coach, played by Tom Hanks, that she is giving up baseball because "It just got too hard." The coach replies, "It's supposed to be hard. If it wasn't hard, everyone would do it. The hard...is what makes it great."[1] As I write that, I can see the scene playing in my head and I think it's so fantastic. Sometimes a hobby or interest requires hard work and a specific set of skills. Sometimes it requires patience, persistence, dedication, and long hours. But that makes it all the more rewarding. "It's the hard that makes it great."

Our interests and hobbies set us apart from those around us and make us distinctive and even exceptional. It would be a pretty boring world if everyone just liked the same things. We are drawn to people with common interests, so we can discuss those interests and learn from each other. My running buddies and I can discuss running for days on end. But when I try to discuss running with my non-running buddies they quickly tire of the subject. I chose running as an interest for a particular reason, stuck with it, and discovered it to be rewarding in and of itself. Of all the interests that I tried as a child, one particular in-

---

[1] *A League of Their Own*, Film. Directed by Penny Marshall. Culver City, CA: Sony Pictures, 1992.

terest has stuck with me through the years, although it was stumbled upon quite unintentionally. One interest was fading away and another one was ready to be born. It's funny how life happens that way. This reminds me of a line from a song: "Every new beginning comes from some other beginning's end."[2] And it all happened on the way to ballet…

As I mentioned, my mom would drive me a long way to the ballet studio. Ballet was not an interest that would stand the test of time and survive into my adulthood. However, as fate or chance would have it, one hobby led me to another. On the way to ballet we would always pass by a small quilt store. At first I did not give the store much thought, but I would always notice it out of the corner of my eye. My grandmother had always been into sewing, needlepoint, and knitting—she actually owned a needlepoint shop at one point. Growing up I would watch her working on a sewing project, sitting in her chair with her half-moon spectacles perched on the end of her nose, with the needle and thread weaving in and out, in and out. She had these little sewing scissors that were shaped like a stork, and I loved to play with them and cut the yarn when she let me. As I grew older I began to notice that quilt store on the way to ballet more and more, as there were always beautiful, colorful quilts displayed in the window. My grandmother did not know anything about quilting, and I had never been exposed to it before. One day when I was about eleven-years-old, I asked my mom if we could stop in that store and look around. She agreed, and I will never forget the first time I walked into that store. I can still remember the smell, the sights, and the sounds. Quilts

---

[2] Semisonic, "Closing Time," *Feeling Strangely Fine*, 1998, MCA.

were draped everywhere, and I had never seen works of art more beautiful! My eyes were wide as saucers as I walked around and gazed at the different patterns, fabrics, and quilting supplies. The idea that you could take different fabrics, design them, cut them, arrange them, and sew them together to actually create a quilt was amazing to me! You could actually put something into the world—create something from scratch that did not exist before and now does exist because you made it! Well, that was it. I was hooked. I simply had to learn how to do this, I thought. I have got to know everything about it and make one of these remarkable things myself.

From then on, every time we passed the quilt store on the way to ballet, I would beg my mom to let me go in. I can be pretty stubborn and persistent, so she usually gave in. A lady at the store named Mary began to notice me coming in each week, and she introduced herself. She could see that I was enamored by the quilts, even at my young age, and so she agreed to teach me how to do it. We picked a small four-patch pillow as a beginning project. I chose four fabrics that were red, white and blue with stars. I got the basic supplies that I needed: needles, thread, special rulers, and an adorable little quilting bag to keep it all in. First Mary showed me how to make a template, trace it on the fabric, and cut it out. She taught me that being exact and precise with measurements, tracing, and cutting was essential to your technique. I learned about making a quarter-inch seam all around the squares, how to line them up just right, pin them, and stitch them together. I was surprised to learn that an ironing board was an essential quilting tool, as you have to iron your seams as the squares are pieced together. Each week on the way to ballet, I would stop in, and Mary would show me the next step in the process. I did not have a sewing machine, so I had to do the sewing by hand. It became very obvious to my mom and me that I was becoming more and more interested in the quilting and less interested in ballet. I would look forward to ballet only because I knew the quilt store was on the way. Well, I eventually finished that little four-patch pillow, and I could not have been more proud of my achievement! When I finished it, I was searching the store for my next project, and I saw a pattern for a wall hanging called the Spectrum Quilt. It had all the colors of the spectrum arranged in a geometric pattern. Mary told me that it was a huge step from the basic pillow to this intricate, complex design, but she could see that I was dedicated and agreed to help me. I remember sitting in my junior high school study hall, getting out my triangles and squares from my backpack, and sewing them together under my desk rather than studying, like I was performing an illegal, covert operation.

So the rest, as they say, is history. A quilter was born. I eventually ceased going to dance classes but continued with my quilting. When I was sixteen-years-old, my family moved to Texas, and I found a quilting studio up the street from my house. I began a huge project with a traditional Amish pattern called Trip Around the World. It had hundreds of little squares in it with pink- and purple-flowered fabrics. I still did not own a sewing machine, so I sewed the entire project by hand. It took me nine long months to complete. I became very friendly with the ladies at the quilting studio. They took me under their wing and helped me along, pleased that such a young person was carrying on the tradition of quilting. One day when I was a senior in high school, a lady came into the studio and purchased a brand new sewing machine. She had a very old sewing machine and asked the storeowners if they could find it a good home with someone who needed it. They immediately thought of me, and I was so pleased and excited to now have a machine of my very own! It had never occurred to me to get a sewing machine. It made my whole endeavor to be a quilter more real, somehow, being the owner of my very own sewing machine. It solidified me into the world of quilt making. The ladies in the shop taught me how to use it, and then there was no stopping me.

I no longer live nearby, but to this day I continue to return to that same quilting store. The storeowners remember me, and still offer advice and guidance. I have made many more quilts for myself and for loved ones, and I learned new skills along the way. I don't know why I was drawn to quilting. My mother said that creativity with sewing runs in the family and that I got it from my grandmother. I can't help but wonder though, what if we had not passed the quilt store on the way to ballet? What if I never took ballet, or I took it at another dance studio, which did not pass that store? Why was I compelled to go in to that store? Why did that particular hobby captivate my interest and stir my passion? Did I choose quilting or did it choose me? I don't know whether we choose our hobbies or they choose us, but I do know that I will always be grateful that I found quilting. There was never a doubt that I loved it from the start. I listened to my heart and my gut instinct. That is how you find your interest—you follow your heart.

I don't know how or why, but my path somehow led me toward quilting. Maybe it will lead me toward other hobbies that are yet to be discovered. I choose to empower myself and listen to my heart, for it has already led me toward lifelong interests, and you never know where it may lead you next.

CHAPTER 11:
WHERE THERE'S SMOKE, THERE'S FIRE...MEN

"There are some very cute firemen in my condo right now. They look like they're straight out of the firemen's calendar," I said in a cool, calm voice. I was on the phone with my mother, standing outside my newly purchased condo with my dog in my arms. Mr. June, July, or August was busting open the roof above my front door. My mom shrieked into the phone, "What?! Why are there firemen? What is going on?" You never think a fire is going to happen to you—until it does. And let me tell you, it's no fun.

OK, let me back up. I have done a lot of moving in my day, and I have lived in many different apartments. In 1995, I moved into a dorm in Austin, Texas, to attend the University of Texas. It was the first time out on my own. After my first year at school, I moved back to my parent's house in Houston for the summer. Then I moved back to Austin and lived in a sorority house on west campus. After my second year, I moved into an apartment in west campus for the summer. Then I moved from the apartment back into the sorority house, and after my third year, I moved back home for the summer. Just thinking about all of the packing, moving, unpacking, repacking, moving, and unpacking is exhausting. So for my fourth year at college, I got another apartment with friends and lived there for a year. It was at that time that I applied for an internship to Walt Disney World in Orlando, Florida, and I actually got it! So I packed up my Mustang and drove to Florida. It turns out that Disney World was a fabulous place to visit, but I was not too happy working there. Three weeks later I packed up my Mustang and drove back to Texas. After a month with my parents, I moved back to Austin. I lived in Austin the next two and a half years and moved twice in that time. I worked at a preschool and went back to the university for a year to become a certified teacher. Then I picked up and moved back to Houston for a job opportunity, into a cozy little apartment near Rice Village. In seven years, I had moved more than ten times! So I decided to throw my boxes away, lose the moving company's phone number, and stay there awhile. I lived in that apartment for three whole years—the longest I had lived anywhere since my childhood home.

So I was sitting around in a bar one night, when I was introduced to a single girl who was about my age. She told me about the condo she had just purchased in an area of town called the Heights. She had grown tired of throwing money away in rent and waiting around for Mr. Right to come along, so she bought a property on her own. The thought of buying a place on my own had never occurred to me. But after talking to this girl, I started imagining the idea, and it grew on me. A seed was planted. She said that she did not have a lot of money and had financed it in such a way to make it possible for her to do it on her own. A few weeks later I was looking at properties with a realtor!

On May 31, 2006, I closed on my new condo. The next weekend I moved in with my doggy in tow, and I was officially a homeowner! I had a wonderful feeling of accomplishment and independence. It was an adorable little condo in a lovely, friendly, quiet complex situated in an ideal part of town; it had one bedroom, one bathroom, and a study, and was on the top floor with high vaulted ceilings. Of course, there were things that I wanted to change about the place: a different color paint would be nice, new floors in the bathroom, kitchen, and entry, a microwave hanging above the oven, a ceiling fan with a light in the bedroom, new windows to replace the fogged ones in the study, and strip the wallpaper in the bathroom and kitchen. Not to mention new, modern light fixtures throughout. But I did not have the money to do any of those things, so the first and only thing I did do was replace the tattered plastic blinds on all of the windows with new white wooden blinds. I was off work for the summer, so I spent the next two and a half months decorating my place perfectly, with just the right furniture in just the right places, each candlestick, picture frame, dishtowel, and pillow in the perfect spot. Unlike all of the other places I had lived, this place was actually my own. I owned it. It was all mine!

And then I had a fire. It all started with the hot water heater. It was located on my patio in the storage closet and it decided to quit working one day while I was in the shower—it was a very cold shower, by the way. So I called up the right people and they came and looked at it. A new water heater was installed, and all was well. Until the city code enforcers came by to make sure the new appliance had been installed according to city code regulations. It turns out that the drainage pipe, which runs from the water heater, down the side of the building, and sticks out of the wall by my downstairs neighbors fence, was supposed to be hanging out six inches from the wall. I called the people who had installed the thing, and they came back out to fix the problem. Now when soldering a pipe, certain precautions must be taken to ensure that pipe does not get overheated. I don't know if the guy knew that or was just in a hurry, but he did his job, I signed his yellow slip, and he was on his way. Several minutes later my downstairs neighbor was hollering about smoke coming out of the wall. I looked over my balcony and, indeed, there was smoke pouring out of the crevices in the wall, and the neighbor was wielding her gardening hose, with the water trickling out. If it wasn't so scary, it would have been funny. So, as the old saying goes, where there's smoke, there's fire. Of course, I put my own spin on the old adage: where there's smoke, there's fire...*men*. I called the fire department, and they raced on over, which brings us back to my mother and I standing outside my condo with the dog asking the firemen, "What month are you?"

Apparently, when firemen are putting out a fire, their number-one priority is to get ahead of that fire and work backward; personal property and belongings don't even get a second thought or consideration whatsoever. Don't get me wrong, I was very grateful to the fire department and they not only saved my home, but that of everyone else who shares my building. So I was very lucky that I called the fire department when I did because my condo received no extensive damage as a result of actual flames. It did, however, look like a giant herd of wild elephants had trampled through on their way to the watering hole on the African Savannah. Or perhaps like the Battle of the Bulge had taken place in my living room. And I don't think I could ever in my whole life forget the smell of smoke that had permeated every single item in the condo from the couch to the socks in the closet, and every item between.

So here I was. I was going back to work the following week, and I had just used every penny of my meager salary to buy this condo. I had spent the last few months putting every single picture frame in its perfect place. And now, instead of reveling in the joys of my home and anticipating returning to work, I was standing on the pavement with the dog, as firemen milled around, the downstairs neigh-

bor shrieked about her cat hidden in her back bedroom somewhere, and other neighbors drifted by to get a look and say how sorry they were it had happened to me. Then out of nowhere came these men in suits, sniffing about like hungry foxes, from different insurance agencies, clothes restoration places, and fire and water damage companies saying, "Sign here! Sign here! Just sign your name on this line!" Oh my goodness, I was completely overwhelmed, so I closed my eyes, took a deep breath, and made an Empowering Choice that helped me to see my way through this entire unexpected day and the next three months:
One step at a time.

Life happens. The unexpected happens, and it can strike any day, at any time, and from out of nowhere. Sometimes it's not fair and we don't deserve it. But life happens. One minute everything is blessedly normal and boring, and then all the sudden everything is very complicated, things are spinning out of control, and you are so overwhelmed that you don't know where to begin or how to proceed. You are faced with something you've never had to deal with before. So what do you do? Baby steps. You have to take little baby steps and handle all of it one step at a time, one day at a time, one moment at a time. You have to just roll with the punches because the punches are going to come, sooner or later. Yup. They may take different forms or disguises, but the punches do come. And sometimes the only choice to make is to just roll with them.

When I first walked into my condo after the fire, I saw it and I smelled it and I could not believe it. I was speechless. I had no words. Then my dad looked at me and said, "Sara, it seems bad right now, but trust me. You are going to come out way ahead in the end. Way ahead." I wasn't sure what he meant, but as it turned out he was exactly right. However, it didn't seem that way the very next day, when the fire and water restoration company came storming in like chimney sweeps, boxing up anything and everything that wasn't tied down. Within two hours, every single thing in the condo had been removed—every piece of furniture, every article of clothing, every photograph, and even the refrigerator, washer, and dryer. The condo was totally stripped naked and bare! They did not, however, take medications, toiletries, candles, food, and other assorted items. Those they left in a giant mountainous heap in the dining room. Later on, I had to take many long hours to write down in exact detail a very long list of every single item left behind to be thrown away.

I was provided with a furnished apartment not far from the condo. However, the towering oak trees under which I would walk the dog were filled with extremely large cockroaches. Yes, you read that right. Cockroaches. The apartment came to be known as the roach motel. I actually woke up in the middle of the night with a roach crawling in my hair! I suppose you could say beggars can't be choosers. I had to shop the next day for basic needs, such as a toothbrush, underwear, shampoo, and a towel. It's amazing how little you actually require to get by on when asked to only buy things that you absolutely need.

So a few days after the fire, one of the insurance agents called and told me to meet with the builder over at the condo. The builder? Why would I need to meet with the builder? Well, there was the matter of the gaping holes all over my ceiling where herds of elephants, I mean firemen, did their job. So patch it up and let me move in, what is the big deal? I went over to the condo and met with the builder, who told me that everything was being replaced: the carpet, the paint, the flooring, and the wallpaper. Everything. I was in disbelief. "Replaced?" I said. Well, as it turns out, as long as they were replacing things, I could choose what they would replace it with! I could choose my new carpeting, flooring, and paint colors. I could choose to strip the wallpaper and paint instead. And as long as we're at it, how about installing the microwave, replacing the fogged windows, replacing the light fixtures, and installing the ceiling fan in my bedroom? When I told my dad about my meeting with the builder, he just sat back, crossed his arms, smiled, and said, "See? What did I tell you? Way ahead!"

The next three months were a whirlwind of contacting insurance agents, signing papers, listing items, making phone calls, going back and forth with the builders and contractors, and taking care of fire-related business. It was like my second job. After work I would come home to the roach motel and start my second job of handling business related to the fire. My father is a businessman and former insurance agent so he knew exactly what needed to be done, but he was determined that I was going to learn to take care of business on my own. So every time I called him, I had five more things added to my to-do list. It got to the point where I would call home to talk to my mom, and when dad would say he needed to talk to me I would quickly say that I had to get going! It would all get done eventually, but my mantra was one step at a time, and that was exactly how I was going to handle it. I would not try to tackle everything all at once or I would be completely overwhelmed by it all. I would not think of how my beautiful condo which was all mine, was almost burned to the ground. I would not think of how the fire chief had said that if I had waited only five more minutes before calling them, the roach motel might have been my permanent home sweet home. I would take it one little bitty step at a time. It was not easy. It was not fun. I was forced into a bare-bones apartment with roaches. All of my precious possessions reeked of smoke, and I wondered if they would ever smell normal again. And my smoky, smelly condo was torn apart and looked like a war zone. I can't help but smile and laugh looking back on it now, as I sit in my beautiful, perfect, and adorable condo at my computer, typing this story and loving every inch of my humble abode. But I was not smiling at the time. Not even close. Especially not when that roach was crawling in my hair.

My parents often use the expression, "It was a blessing in disguise." I guess that's what my fire was. Bad things happen, and it can seem like the end of the world. There are so many times when you feel like the walls are caving in all around, and you may feel you'll never recover. But you do recover. You take it one day at a time, and things just have a way of working out. But they don't always work out for themselves. You have to take control of the situation and stand up for yourself. You have to be your own advocate and look out for number one (that would be *you*, in case you don't know that.) You have to empower yourself. You have to roll with the punches and just move forward, one step at a time. You have to look for the positive in the situation and turn your frown upside down. That's how you get to the finish line—one foot in front of the other. And nobody can move your feet for you. Sometimes you get help, but inevitably you've got to go it alone sometimes. When bad things are dropped in your lap, you've got to pick yourself up off the floor, and keep going because you just never know.

Despite everything, you could come out ahead in the end—way ahead.

CHAPTER 12:
A CALL TO ACTION

Now this is a call to action! So get on out there and *empower* yourself ladies and gentlemen! And don't be wishy-washy about it! Don't say, "Oh, I think I'll *try* to eat better" or "Oh, I think I'll *try* to be more confident." You can't just choose a random desire and say you'll *try* it. That's not what Empowering Choices are. If you think that's what it is, you need to flip back to page one. Empowering Choices stem from the circumstances in your life, and they are *not* something that you just *try*! In the words of Yoda, "Do or not do. There is no try."[1]

The definition of empower is *to give power or authority to* or *to authorize.*[2] When you make an Empowering Choice, you are finding that power within yourself. It's in there. It really is. You just have to believe in yourself, find the power, and harness it. You are taking ownership of yourself and your life. You are giving authority to yourself and authorizing yourself to take control of a situation, make a choice, and stick to your guns. In the beginning of this book, I said that an Empowering Choice is a single decision, in a single moment that you make for yourself. You are absolutely positive and have no doubt that it is the right choice for you. The decision to stick to this choice, to not waver in your conviction, and to stand up for its rightness and goodness is what makes it an Empowering Choice and not an ordinary choice. When I decided to never have a shot in the toe ever again, I empowered myself. I took control of my destiny. When I decided to earn a college degree, I

---

[1] *The Empire Strikes Back*, Film. Directed by Irvin Kershner. Lucasfilm. 20th Century Fox, 1980.
[2] Collins English Dictionary. Complete and Unabridged 6th Edition 2003. HarperCollins Publishers, 2003.

empowered myself. When I decided to be a runner and to not give up in the face of a running injury, I empowered myself. When I decided to be a whole person, to have a sausage (I mean, a baby) someday, to not be a victim, and to listen to my voice I empowered myself. When I chose to follow my heart toward the interests I wanted to pursue, I made an Empowering Choice. When I had a fire in my condo, I empowered myself by taking things one step at a time.

When I decided to beat the bridge, I made a choice that empowered me and inspired me. I authorized myself to take control and look out for number one. Number one is *me*. It reminds me of a poem:
"For it isn't your father or mother or wife,
Whose judgment upon whom you must pass.
The fellow whose verdict counts most in your life
Is the one staring back from the glass."[3]

Always remember that. You come first and foremost, before anybody else. I know that there will be many more obstacles and challenges and choices to make in life. There will be bridges to beat. I will make the best decisions I can make for myself and live with the consequences. I will trust myself that I know what is best for me. I will do whatever it takes to beat those bridges if, in my heart of hearts, I know that it is what I must do.

You might be thinking: where do I start? Think about choices you have made in your own life. You may discover that you have already made Empowering Choices of your own. Sometimes there are moments in our lives when we make decisions, and we don't realize at the time how

---

[3] Peter "Dale" Wimbrow, "The Man in the Glass," *The American Magazine* (1934).

important they will turn out to be. We don't realize how everything went in a certain direction as a result of that choice and everything would have gone differently had we chosen something else. We have regrets. If only I had chosen this path and not that path. I believe that it is never too late to choose the right path. There are many people out there who are facing much bigger problems than me. There are many people who are frying much bigger fish and trying to beat challenging bridges. But there is always an Empowering Choice to make. It may be as simple as having hope and reminding yourself every morning that there is hope. Or it may be writing down one thing each day that you like about yourself, or one good thing that happened today. It may be promising to take things one step at a time. So where do you start? You start by getting a journal. Get a blank book to collect your thoughts in and write down your feelings. Maybe you have one lying around the house. If you don't have one, go to the nearest bookstore and get one. Go ahead. I'll wait here.

Got it? Okay, now what are your non-negotiables? What are you facing? What obstacles have you overcome in your life and how did you overcome them? What do you love about yourself? What do you want to change? What are specific steps you can take to change? What forks in the road do you have in your life? Do you have crutches that you are depending on to stand up or to move forward? What is preventing you from standing on your own two feet? Are you surrounding yourself with people and situations that are good for you, or toxic? Are you ignoring opportunities that are staring you in the face? Are you not where you want to be in your life but blaming others rather than yourself? What can you control? What is out of your control? Take a look in the mirror—a good, hard look.

And write it down. Get a pen, pencil, marker, or whatever you have and write it. Don't type these things on the computer, but actually physically write them. There's something about writing things out with a pen that helps you own up to things and see the cold, hard, undeniable truth. So get on out there and empower yourself! To steal a line from Dr. Seuss "Your mountain is waiting!"[4]

When I first walked into Dr. Kieke's office, I saw a poster of basketball player extraordinaire Michael Jordan on the wall. When I was growing up, my brother idolized Michael Jordan. He had a poster of him hanging on the wall that read: "This man does not come from earth. He only visits for games and practices." In fact, my brother contended that Michael Jordan was God himself. I don't know much about basketball, but I do know that there are people who say that Jordan is the best basketball player there ever was. On the poster in Dr. Kieke's office there was a quote that read:

> "I have missed more than 9000 shots in my career. I have lost almost 300 games. On 26 occasions I have been entrusted to take the game winning shot...and missed. And I have failed over and over and over again in my life. And that is why I succeed."[5]

I saw that poster day after day, week after week, month after month when I went into Dr. K's office for therapy. I never gave it much thought. Then one day I was waiting, staring at it, and it hit me. This was Michael Jordan. The Best. The man my brother said was God. And he failed? Over and over?! He was entrusted with the game winning

---
[4] *Oh, the Places You'll Go!*. Deluxe/Slipcase ed. New York: Random House Books for Young Readers, 1993.
[5] Michael Jordan, American NBA Basketball Player, b.1963.

shot twenty-six times and missed? That number was rather ironic because it's the number of miles in a marathon. The poster said that he failed over and over and over and that is why he succeeded. How does failing over and over and over make you succeed? That did not add up to me. I try. I fail. I try. I fail. I try. I fail. How does that equal success? What if you keep trying, you keep failing, and you never win? What if I keep trying to run, and I keep ending up sitting in this office in pain? How does continued failure equal success? I just didn't get it.

After more than a year of therapy at Dr. K's office, I began training for the Marine Corps Marathon again. I was finally on my way after so much pain, so many doctors, so many hours of therapy, icing, heating, stretching, strengthening, and soreness. It was four months into my training and everything was going well. There had been a few minor tweaks that I had worked out but I was getting through all of my workouts and long runs with success. Then my left leg starting acting up. It started in my hip and glute, and pretty much spread to the whole leg. Here we go again!! I could not believe it. The first time around the injury was in my right leg and now it was starting in my left. Dr. K said I should run loops in the park and do half of my long runs aqua jogging in the pool. He assured me that it would still be okay for the marathon. He assured me that aqua jogging would keep up my conditioning. He assured me that it was a small bump in the road. He knew by then that I was a person who needs a lot of reassurance!

The next Saturday, I was running loops in the park. I had not been able to run with my regular running group, as I had done every Saturday since the beginning of the training season, because of the pain in my left leg. After all I had gone through, I was back here again, in pain again.

I thought it was the beginning of the end for me. I would have to cancel my flight to Washington, DC, cancel my hotel reservation, defer my marathon registration, and dedicate all of my free time for at least another year, possibly longer, to this endeavor. I was trudging along, feeling it in my leg with every single step, staring down at the ground in defeat. There was a runner in front of me with a white shirt on. It was nothing out of the ordinary. But something made me glance up and look at his shirt. On the back it read: Fall Seven Times; Stand Up Eight.[6] I stopped dead in my tracks. The person behind me almost ran into me and said, "Hey, watch out!" I just stood there. I kept repeating it in my head over and over and over.

Fall seven times; stand up eight.
Fall seven times; stand up eight.
Fall seven times; stand up eight.

This is a sign, I thought. This is just what I needed, I thought. This is my new motto for life, I thought. Where does it come from? Who originated this saying? I didn't know, and I didn't care; I knew that it was what I had to do. I fall, and I stand up. I fall again and I stand up again. One time, three times, seven times, or a hundred times makes no difference. I stand up, and I press on. As Kevin Cronin of REO Speedwagon says, "Even if you think your strength is gone, keep pushin' on."[7] Ironically, Dr. K was doctor number eight for me and the one who helped me so my new motto was especially appropriate. I went online and ordered a necklace with the saying on it. I told the jewelry company that it was very important that I get it right

---

[6] Japanese Proverb
[7] REO Speedwagon, "Keep Pushin'," *The Essential REO Speedwagon*, 1976, Sony Music Entertainment, Inc.

away. My silver necklace arrived two days later with the inscription.

The next week I was back in Dr. K's office staring back at "God," I mean, Michael Jordan. I read that last line on the poster again: *And I have failed over and over and over again in my life. And that is why I succeed.* A light bulb went off in my brain. It was just like my new motto. He succeeded because each time he failed, he got back out there and tried again. He would not give in to failure. Each time he missed the winning shot or lost the game, he got back out there and tried again. Each time he fell, he stood up. My new motto was exactly what Michael Jordan was saying. That is how you succeed. It makes no difference if you win or lose in the end. It's the fact that you would not give up. I have a picture that I got at the running expo in Washington, DC hanging up in my condo that reads, "It is not the race that makes you a winner; it is what leads up to the race that determines your success."[8] That goes for everything in life, of course, not just running. If you have the courage to start in the first place and to keep on going through hail, wind, rain, or storms, then you have already succeeded. You have all the tools that you need right inside of you. You are everything that you need. Choose it—choose to be everything that you need.

I am not perfect, and I do not always make the right choices. I don't always make choices that are empowering. My glass is not always half full, and I do not always practice what I preach. Sometimes I want to give up, and it just feels easier to sit back on the couch, take the easy road, and let life pass me by. Sometimes I compare myself to others who have it better than I do, and I say, "It's just

---
[8] Janice Earhart, "The Race," iZoar, 2008

not fair!" Sometimes I am negative and pessimistic. Sometimes I have pity parties and wallow in my own sorrows. But hey, there is nothing wrong with that. Everyone deserves to wallow now and then and everyone deserves a pity party. But like Scarlett O'Hara says when Rhett Butler leaves her at the end of *Gone With the Wind*, "I'll find some way to get him back. After all, tomorrow is another day!"[9] There is another day, and the sun will rise tomorrow. That is a certainty. It is never too late to make an Empowering Choice and turn things around. It is never too late.

One of my favorite movie quotes comes from the movie *Cast Away* with Tom Hanks. Tom Hanks's character was stranded on an island for four years after a plane crash and is talking to his friend after his rescue. He says:

"I knew, somehow, that I had to stay alive. Somehow. I had to keep breathing. Even though there was no reason to hope. And all my logic said that I would never see this place again. So that's what I did. I stayed alive. I kept breathing. And one day my logic was proven all wrong because the tide came in, and gave me a sail. And now, here I am. I'm back. In Memphis, talking to you. I have ice in my glass…and I know what I have to do now. I gotta keep breathing. Because tomorrow the sun will rise. Who knows what the tide could bring?"[10]

Life is funny that way. You never know where your path will lead you. You just never know. Lightning can strike. So even though it's hard sometimes to keep going and not give up, I realize that I have to. Like Tom Hanks's

---

[9] *Gone with the Wind*, Film. Directed by Victor Fleming. Burbank: Warner Home Video, 1939.
[10] *Cast Away*, Film. Directed by Robert Zemeckis. Tucson: 20th Century Fox, 2000.

character in *Cast Away*, I have to keep going, and I have to empower myself because nobody else is going to do it for me. It's all up to me.

Not long after I completed the Marine Corps Marathon in October 2009, I was at a luncheon at my cousin's house. There were some people there that I had not seen since my injury was at its worst. One person asked if I was still running, and before I could answer another said, "I thought you gave that up. You quit."

I just shook my head and said, "Nope. I'm not the quittin' kind."

Made in the USA
Charleston, SC
07 June 2010